SOCIALISM IN BRITAIN

THE MEN AND IDEAS SERIES
General Editor: R. W. Harris

THE FIRST THREE VOLUMES:

TUDOR ECONOMIC PROBLEMS
by Peter Ramsey

POLITICAL IDEAS 1760-1792
by R. W. Harris

THE LIBERAL PARTY FROM
EARL GREY TO ASQUITH
by R. B. McCallum

By the same author:

WILLIAM MARSHAL (Blackwell)

THROUGH SOVIET RUSSIA (Houghton Publishing Co)

TURKEY (Arrowsmith)

THE EUROPEAN WORLD 1870-1945
(with Dr T. K. Derry) (Bell)

LANDMARKS IN THE HISTORY OF EDUCATION
(John Murray)

THE RISE AND FALL OF NAZI GERMANY (Cresset Press)

THE MAKING OF MODERN BRITAIN
(with Dr T. K. Derry) (John Murray)

DEMOCRACY AND WORLD CONFLICT (Blandford)

For Children:

GREAT BRITAIN (with Dr T. K. Derry)
(Oxford University Press, Toronto)

PICTURE HISTORY OF ITALY (Oxford University Press)

THE MEN AND IDEAS SERIES

SOCIALISM IN BRITAIN

*From the Industrial Revolution
to the Present Day*

by

T. L. JARMAN

Reader in Education, University of Bristol

TAPLINGER PUBLISHING COMPANY
NEW YORK

First published in the United States in 1972 by
TAPLINGER PUBLISHING CO., INC.
New York, New York

Copyright© 1972 by T. L. JARMAN
All rights reserved.
Printed in Great Britain

Library of Congress Catalog Card Number: 73-185255
ISBN 0-8008- 7240-1

CONTENTS

PREFACE

THE THEME OF this book is the rise and decline of socialism in Britain. In writing on a controversial subject of this kind it is probably desirable that the author should declare his own political allegiance. I have always been a Liberal, but one who has felt at times the attraction of the socialist ideal without being able to accept it as a system.

I am grateful to the University of Bristol for allowing me time to complete the book, and especially to Professor Roger Wilson who arranged this for me, and who also read and criticised some of my chapters. Many years ago my interest in the subject was stimulated by discussions with G. D. H. Cole and Harold Laski, and I was fortunate to have been at New College, Oxford in the days of the future Labour ministers, Hugh Gaitskell and Mr Crossman and Mr Jay.

I am grateful also for their ready help to Mr E. Brown, librarian of the TUC library in Bloomsbury, and to Mrs I. Wagner, librarian at the Labour Party headquarters in Transport House.

Mr R. W. Harris, editor of the series in which this book appears, helped me very much with his encouragement in the early stages, and my publishers have offered me valuable suggestions. Dr T. B. Caldwell, of Leeds University, and Dr J. T. Ward, of Strathclyde University, were both kind enough to read my early chapters and give me the benefit of their knowledge and criticism. At Bristol, I thank in particular Mr George Sakwa, who read my later chapters and criticised them in detail, and also Mr Edward David, who pointed me to some helpful information. But of course, I alone am responsible for the way I have used their advice and for any expressions of opinion.

The bibliography lists the books I have used and their publishers. For the discussion of socialism in recent years I must acknowledge my use of *The Socialist Case* by the Rt Hon Douglas Jay (Faber), *Nationalised Industry and Public Ownership* by Professor W. A. Robson (Allen & Unwin), *Nationalisation in Britain* by R. Kelf-Cohen (Macmillan), *New Fabian Essays* edited by the Rt Hon R. H. S. Crossman (Turnstile Press), *The Future of Socialism* by the Rt Hon C. A. R. Crosland (Cape), *Fabian Tracts*, and *The God That Failed* by Arthur Koestler and others (Hamish Hamilton). Grateful acknowledgment is made for permission to quote certain passages.

I should also like to thank Mrs K. Matthews and Mrs Johnson who typed the manuscript.

T. L. JARMAN

INTRODUCTION:

Socialism—its Meaning and Background

W HEN THE LABOUR Party gained power for the first time by its resounding victory in the general election of 1945, at the close of the Second World War, it must have seemed that at last socialism was to be firmly established as a political system. But the ups and downs in its fortunes during the coming quarter of a century were to demonstrate the uncertainties of political fortune, and, even during the election campaign, some of the uncertainties of socialism's past were to emerge. Winston Churchill, the Conservative leader, spoke of the socialist doctrine as "this continental conception of human society called socialism, or in its more violent form communism"—and went on to declare that "no socialist system can be established without a political police—some form of *Gestapo*". To which the Labour leader, C. R. Attlee, responded that Churchill had forgotten that "socialist theory was developed by Robert Owen in Britain long before Karl Marx", and that the British countries of Australia and New Zealand had had socialist government for years without the dreadful consequences that the Conservative leader forecast. The confrontation of the two political leaders over a question of general principle was somewhat unusual—for principles, as *The Times* pointed out, are of less concern to the electorate than bread-and-butter matters. The issue, however, was one of real interest. Question after question springs into mind. What is socialism? What is communism? Is communism the same thing as socialism, simply another name for it? Did these political doctrines come from the Continent, with Karl Marx? Or is there a native British socialism to be traced back to Owen, whom Marx dismissed as utopian? Do the protagonists of different forms of socialism agree, perhaps, on the end but disagree as to the means? On the Continent, would the secret police be the natural means, whereas in this country more gentlemanly means might be appropriate?

Robert Owen and Karl Marx were both present in Paris in 1848, that year of revolutions, one stage in the series of revolutions which started with the French Revolution of 1789. Owen and Marx were there, but there is no record that they ever met. Their doctrines had common elements, they took shape at the same time, but they diverged; like their propounders they did not meet. And their divergence led to a dichotomy in socialism which has never ceased to influence the movement profoundly, both in its theories and their interpretation but also in their application : socialism by revolution on the one hand, evolutionary or parliamentary socialism on the other.

Both Churchill and Attlee had a claim to be right about the origins of socialism, but about British socialism Attlee was nearer the truth. Continental socialism, on which Churchill chose to focus attention, found its more immediate origin in the scientific socialism of Karl Marx and its application in the Soviet experiment after the Russian Revolution of 1917; British socialism, on the other hand, was not deeply influenced by Marxism, could trace a line of development back to Robert Owen, and had its own special nature moulded by the evolving democracy of the British political system, the respectable tradition of nonconformity, and the tolerance and love of compromise which came to appear as almost inborn features of the national character.

Robert Owen, in spite of Marx's disparagement in dismissing the Owenites as utopian, put his finger on the basic and essential feature of socialism. In fact, the first definition —and effective and clear at that—is to be found in an

Owenite publication of 1827. The writer, discussing the labour and capital which go into the production of commodities, says that the main question is "whether it is more beneficial that this capital should be individual or common". Those who thought the former were the economists, James Mill, Malthus, and so on; those who thought it should be common were "the communists and socialists". This appears to be the first use of the term socialist, and the writer has gone right to the heart of the matter—public ownership or control of capital, what became much later, in the words of the Labour Party constitution, "the common ownership of the means of production, distribution, and exchange". And socialism usually implies—as is indicated by the word "beneficial" in the Owenite definition—social justice, equitable division of wealth, and international peace. There is not, originally, any clear difference between socialist and communist, although the term communist is now generally used to describe those who seek to achieve socialism by revolutionary means. Owen himself was clear about the underlying character of the new socialist idea which was taking shape : "the principle of union and co-operation is superior to the individual selfish system", and, writing in 1825 at his community of New Harmony in the United States, he declared : "In fact the whole of this country is ready to commence a new empire upon the principle of public property and to discard private property." He had indeed indicated the Socialist principle; but he was over-optimistic as to the possibilities and the length of time required for putting it into practice. Again and again Owenites contrast the ruling competitive system of economics with their own co-operative political economy. The contrast was stressed between wealth and misery, the paradox of poverty in the midst of plenty. Owen realised that machinery was putting a new power into man's hands; he calculated that in the short period of twenty-five years between 1792 and 1817 the productive capacity per head in Great Britain had increased twelve times. Owen declared that society had "passed a boundary never before reached in the history of man", poverty was no longer necessary, the co-operative organisation of machine production would bring abundance. There was at last a practical basis for the happiness of all. Indeed one might have felt that the modern Labour Party was about to take control of a situation, already clearly analysed by Owen, when Attlee formulated his message to the Labour candidates of 1945 : "We propose in the interests of the whole nation that the community should become the master of its economic progress and prosperity, instead of leaving control in private hands to be used primarily for the private advantage of a few."

Owen and the Owenites indicated the essential character of socialism : the control of economic power for the public good. Marx and the Marxists indicated what they considered the necessary method: the revolutionary seizure of power by the working class. But, of course, behind these modern doctrines there is a long history, the history of socialism. There is, in every age, a certain interest among men in political and economic matters; the particular form this interest takes will depend on the actual conditions and circumstances of the age, and on the special idiosyncrasies and background of the individuals who give lasting expression to the political interest. Owen saw his idea of a socialist community as "founded upon a principle commended by Plato, Lord Bacon, Sir Thomas More, and R. Owen"; it had its antecedents in the ideas of past thinkers. The ideas of such thinkers and many others form an important part—perhaps the most important part—of the history of socialism; they make up the theory of the movement. But one can observe also, from time to time, attempts actually to set up communities on such a basis that their worldly goods and productive effort could be organised for the common good. And one sees, too, in every age more violent movements : risings of slaves and slave wars in the ancient world of Greece and

Rome, peasant revolts in medieval Europe, revolutionary changes of government and seizing of power in modern times. In many of these there was a socialistic element. But not until the Russian Revolution of 1917 did socialists anywhere succeed in seizing economic power and establishing a socialist state.

Plato and Aristotle do indeed, among the Greeks, provide an early and vivid introduction to social problems still of fundamental concern. Plato's *Republic*, the first and most famous in a long succession of utopian works which give expression to man's dream of an ideal state, has as its basis the idea of community or communism. The state, as Plato visualised it, was to be ruled by a governing class of guardians, specially selected and trained for the purpose. The guardians were to live under a communistic system, for "friends have all things in common". Whether the communistic system was only for the guardians or was to apply also to the ordinary people of the state, is not quite clear. But as the guardians were the ruling element their communistic system would naturally set the tone of the whole society. Plato's communism was far-reaching and complete. It involved community of property : no one was to have anything specially his or her own, and men and women were to live in common houses and would meet at common meals. It involved also equality of the sexes : women were to be rulers like men, and were to have the same education as men, in music, gymnastics, and military exercises. And, most striking of all, it involved community of wives and children : there was to be no individual marriage, as we know it; instead there would be a regulated system of breeding through sacred marriage festivals. Good would be paired with good to produce the best offspring; and only the best would be reared, the weak or ill being destroyed. The children would be brought up in common nurseries, and care would be taken that no mother should recognise her own children. It was, indeed, a rigorous and thorough system which only a theorist, perhaps, could suggest—but it had its counterparts, partially, in the discipline and common life of Sparta, in the exposure of weakly infants which was an accepted practice in ancient Greece, and, in modern times, in the idea of regulated breeding and control to develop a master race which was revived in Nazi Germany. And Owenites realised that the individual family was a real obstacle to the organisation of community.

Plato suggested his system of communism because he saw the great evils of discord, disagreement, and distraction which existed in states; the greatest good in the state, he said, was unity. This unity would exist where there were no private interests, pleasures, or pains. This argument might be taken in a general way, without definite reference to the specifically socialist feature of community in the economic sense, of common property. But Plato did seek to avoid the social and economic division in other states—"For indeed", he says, "any city is in fact divided into two, one the city of the poor, the other of the rich; these are at war with one another"—and in this he is pointing out the class war over two thousand years before Karl Marx. Other advantages of the communistic system, Plato thought, would be that the guardians, having no private interests to distract them, would remain devoted to the public interest, there would be no lawsuits about property, the sickening flattery of the rich would disappear, there would be no borrowing and failing to repay, and women would be freed from sordid household cares and men able to devote their full energy to affairs of state.

Aristotle, in his *Politics*, answered Plato's arguments for a communistic organisation of society. To Plato's contention, "the greater the unity of the state the better", Aristotle replied that there could be too much unity; it was important to preserve the differentiation of functions which naturally exists among men. As for the community of wives and children, such an arrangement would destroy natural affection;

in trying to bring about an all-embracing unity within the state, Plato's system would destroy an existing and real bond of sympathy between people—thus it would, in effect, tend to bring the reverse of Plato's aim. The bond between husband and wife, parent and child, is real and in this it makes for unity—this real bond of unity would disappear if Plato's system were to come into existence. "Of the two qualities which chiefly inspire regard and affection—that a thing is your own and that you love it—neither can exist in such a state as this."

Certainly all the weight of experience suggests that Aristotle was right about this; the enduring strength of the marriage relationship and of family affection and interests are matters of common observation, whereas devotion to the community, except perhaps in time of war, is very much weaker. When it came to community of property, Aristotle once more had his feet firmly on the ground. Abolition of property, Aristotle maintained, was impractical. "For that which is common to the greatest number has the least care bestowed upon it. Everyone thinks chiefly of his own, hardly at all of the common interest; and only when he is himself concerned as an individual." And this argument in favour of private property has been used ever since—from Aristotle to the *Daily Telegraph* or the *Daily Mail*. As in the case of the family relationship, it is one which ordinary experience and observation bear out. Man takes great pleasure in feeling that a thing is his own. "The love of self," said Aristotle, "is a feeling implanted by nature and not given in vain." The evils which men suppose to arise from private property are, he said, "due to a very different cause—the wickedness of human nature". Evil men may abuse the institution of property, but they would also find ways of abusing the institution of communism. When men improve, their use of property will improve also—something approaching communism might come about. "Friends will have all things in common," Plato had said. Men will have all things in common *when* they are friends, would represent Aristotle's view. But this is doubtless a distant ideal: Communism brought about by free will would still appear to be utopian, brought about by force, as experience since 1917 has shown us, it is barbarism.

Plato has never failed to exercise a peculiar fascination, offering lines of thought from which conclusions can be drawn from either side, liberal or totalitarian; Aristotle, though less often quoted, affords a powerful corrective. These two writers state so clearly the arguments for and against community of property that one wonders why so many others have had to take up and repeat the arguments—but each age feels it necessary to make its own restatement of old ideas. Many writers over the centuries have tried to portray—like Plato—an ideal state. Concerned with such a task—and some involving an element of socialism—are Cicero's *De Republica*, St Augustine's *De Civitate Dei*, Dante's *De Monarchia*, Sir Thomas More's *Utopia*—which has given a name to this kind of literature, Lord Bacon's *New Atlantis*, and Campanella's *City of the Sun*. In this way the origins of socialist and communist thought can be traced back to the ancient world, and its development observed through the ages.

Both in the early days of the Christian Church and in the society of the Middle Ages which grew up under the influence of the church, there were elements of socialism. These elements have been ignored by some, exaggerated by others; over-sentimentalised, perhaps, yet they are of great interest in themselves, and illustrate the continuing concern with questions of property and with the control of economic life. The teaching of Christ had in it a strong communistic character, a stress on the values of poverty and simplicity—"Blessed are the poor"; "Ye cannot serve God and Mammon"; "Go and sell that thou hast, and give to the poor"; and, "It is easier for a camel to go through the eye of a needle, than for a rich man to enter into the Kingdom

of God". The early Christian communities lived according
to communistic principles. As the *Acts of the Apostles* put
it : "And all that believed were together, and had all things
common; and they sold their possessions and goods, and
parted them to all, according as every man had need". The
writings of the Fathers of the Church, both Greek and
Latin, in the early centuries after Christ built up a strong
tradition in favour of a communistic and ascetic way of life.
But in spite of the Christian teaching and spirit, the world
remained dominant. And the Church itself became worldly;
it acquired wealth, power, organisation—it became an institution. To escape from the world, from its wealth, its
material trappings, and its uncertainties, earnest Christians
would renounce all worldly goods and become hermits. Later
the withdrawal from the world became organised in monas-
ticism. St Benedict set up the monastery of Monte Cassino in
529, with its rules of manual labour, chastity, and obedience.
Other orders followed during the Middle Ages. But the
monasteries themselves acquired lands and wealth; great
abbots, like bishops, were comparable with nobles. Once
more the spirit was lost in an institution; power and wealth
usurped the place of poverty and simplicity. So much so,
that tension grew up between the church as an institution
and those within it who clung to the principle of evangelical
poverty. And so those who went too far in their support
of this principle came to be condemned as heretics by the
institution, and the long and bitter struggles with Waldenses,
Cathars, Lollards followed, struggles which were forerunners
of the conflicts of the Reformation.

The monastery was itself an organisation whose rules and
way of life demonstrated the possibility of running a society
or community on communistic principles. The driving force
was religious belief, and it is noteworthy that these religious
communities were far more numerous, more successful, and
more lasting than the Owenite communities of the nineteenth

century which were founded on purely social and rational principles.

In the Middle Ages, when the influence of the church was dominant, economic life was regulated, at least to some extent, by Christian principles, and since Christian teaching was often directed against riches, and in favour of poverty, there was inevitably in medieval economic life a socialistic or communistic note. The church, in spite of early teaching and practice, came to accept and justify private property. St Thomas Aquinas, the author of the most authoritative statement of medieval Christian doctrine, maintained that, whereas community of goods might be appropriate in the ideal condition of nature before Adam's fall, in a wicked, fallen world private property was necessary. Aquinas, in addition, borrowed from Aristotle his arguments in favour of property. But though property was regarded as lawful, the property-owner had his responsibilities: he must give alms to the poor, and if he did not do so he would be guilty of sin. In the same way the church looked with suspicion on great wealth made by trade. There was, it was held, a just price for any article; this was a price sufficient to cover the cost of material and labour, and sellers should not take advantage of a temporary shortage to raise prices. Usury, or the taking of interest on loans, was condemned. Such condemnation was justifiable, so long as loans were in the nature of help to tide over a temporary distress. But as time went on, loans were increasingly made to merchants or business men who used the loan to make a profit. In such cases, the lender was justified in taking his share, and the church, though uneasy about high rates of interest, was forced to modify its position. In the craft guilds, also, there was a socialistic element. The guild fixed prices with the intention of protecting the buyer and also securing a fair return for his labour to the producer.

The Peasants' Revolt of 1381 in England was partly a demand for definite material improvements in their position,

partly a rising with a more general communistic character.
The peasants asked to be rid of villeinage, to be free of
manorial services and to pay instead a yearly rent, and to
see the end of such obligations as having to grind their corn
at the lord's mill. But Wyclif's onslaught on the worldliness
of the church could be used to justify an attack on church
property, and the idea of an ideal state of man before the
fall encouraged people to think that land ought to be divided
equally among the peasants. John Ball's communistic sermons
played their part, and the famous couplet went from mouth
to mouth :

> When Adam delved and Eve span,
> Where was then a gentleman?

This was indeed a heady wine for the peasants, but their
revolt failed.

Such ideas, however, had a wide appeal, and not unnaturally, to simple people. They showed themselves again
in the seventeenth century. In the disturbed conditions of the
Commonwealth period there was a movement of agrarian
communism associated with the Levellers or Diggers. In
1649 Winstanley and his followers began to dig up and
plant St George's Hill in Surrey. Troops were called to dis-
perse them, and once again the vision of a communist
utopia dissolved. During the Thirty Years War in Germany
the Anabaptists of Munster put into force a communistic
regime of an extreme character—but only for a short time
and under exceptional circumstances.

During the eighteenth century in France, the period of
the Enlightenment, the *philosophes* made fundamental and
far-reaching criticisms of the society of their day. Those
most remembered are Voltaire and Rousseau. Their publications doubtless did something to weaken the stability of
the *ancien régime* in France, but their arguments were of

a political—liberal or democratic—rather than of an economic nature. Revolutions there were, in America and in
France, but the revolutions were political—they resulted in
changes of government, as had done the English revolutions
of the preceding century. Important as these changes were,
there was in no case any fundamental change in the ownership and control of wealth and economic power as a whole.
In France, the revolutionary demands were summed up as
"Liberty, Equality, Fraternity". Liberty meant freedom from
despotic government, equality meant equality before the law
(rather than equality of property), and fraternity meant—
what indeed? Brotherhood?—but was there more brotherhood, or less, after the twenty years of war which followed
the French Revolution and the Terror? There were also,
however, in eighteenth century France undercurrents of
socialism. Socialistic or communistic anticipations may be
found in the writings of Morelly, Mably, and Meslier. In
Rousseau's essay on the origin of inequality there was an
attack on the evils of private property. And the grievances
of which the French representatives complained at the
Estates General in 1789 were often as much economic as
political.

The leaders of the French Revolution—both moderates
and extremists—for the most part upheld private property;
they were not socialists or communists. They stood for breaking up the great estates and ending the property rights of
the church, but this was to diffuse property-owning, not to
destroy it. Nevertheless, during the Revolution the social
question was forced to the front by the menacing conflict
between rich and poor : in the countryside the peasants
sacked the country houses of the landed nobles, burnt title-
deeds, and seized the land. In the towns, the working class
began to organise itself, but if it gained anything it was
merely citizenship not property. Nothing in the nature of
socialism followed. There was, however, one attempt by a
small group to put into practice by force the principles of

community of property. This was probably the first clear and definite attempt in history at a communist seizure of power; it followed the fall of the Jacobin extremists, and the reaction which set in against the Revolution under the new government known as the Directory. The attempt was the conspiracy of Gracchus Babeuf in 1796 : it aimed at seizing economic power by putting an end to private property, and at using the dictatorship of the proletariat to safeguard and maintain its position. The conspiracy had no large following; it found its supporters only in Paris and the larger towns—the peasants who had already acquired land were certainly unwilling to support a movement aimed at community of property. The conspiracy failed, and Babeuf was executed. But one conspirator, Buonarotti, who survived, wrote later a full account of the affair, and his book was much used by revolutionaries in the following decades, and influenced the development of revolutionary theory. Babeuf's conspiracy came to be regarded by socialists and communists as the first example of the proletariat in action.

Ideas and action—socialism in theory, and attempts to put something better in place of the existing order—these things were not new. But it was the Industrial Revolution at the end of the eighteenth and beginning of the nineteenth century in Britain which first brought socialism into the forefront of practical concern. Even then it was a long time— upwards of a century—before major events took place. The Industrial Revolution stimulated a criticism of the economic theory of capitalism, and at the same time brought an attack on the social conditions which the new factories had created. Socialism—co-operation instead of competition—was seen as the solution. It was not, however, until the twentieth century that the organisation of nation-wide socialist parties made possible the election of socialist governments to power and that, in one country in 1917, a revolutionary seizure of power established a communist state.

PART I

The Working Class is Born: Beginnings of British Socialism

1. The Industrial Revolution

THE INDUSTRIAL REVOLUTION is not merely a convenient starting place for a study of socialism in modern Britain; it is fundamental to such a study. For nothing is more certain to give rise to new ways of thought than a threat to man's livelihood and way of life—nothing, that is, except such a threat accompanied by some ray of hope, some promise of salvation, some doctrine indicating a way out and a happy solution. The French Revolution let loose a flood of new ideas, heady ideas like strong wine—liberty, equality, brotherhood, the career open to talents, and with them undercurrents of socialism. A better world seemed within man's grasp. Something of the feeling of the times was expressed by Wordsworth:

> Bliss was it in that dawn to be alive,
> But to be young was very heaven!

And idealists and enthusiasts were inspired and called to work

> Not in Utopia . . .
> But in the very world, which is the world
> Of all of us—the place where, in the end,
> We find our happiness, or not at all!

The ideas and sentiments of the French Revolution had their effect in Britain, too, yet meanwhile the inexorable forces of economic change, which made the Industrial Revolution, were transforming men's lives, giving to some the opportunity to make great wealth, but bringing to others disaster and unemployment when old domestic crafts declined, and to others yet again employment in the new factories, but for long hours at low wages. Poverty and misery was the lot of many in a period of rapid and unregulated economic change. To Shelley, at the time of Peterloo, the lot of the poor under their capitalist masters was slavery—and what was this slavery?

> 'Tis to let the Ghost of Gold
> Take from Toil a thousandfold
> More than e'er its substance could
> In the tyrannies of old. . . .
>
> And at length when ye complain
> With a murmur weak and vain
> 'Tis to see the Tyrant's crew
> Ride over your wives and you—
> Blood is on the grass like dew.'

Historians, like mankind in general, are not immune from changes of fashion. The terms, French Revolution and Industrial Revolution, which for long enough appeared clear and satisfactory, have more recently been criticised. The first can be shown to be part of a wider, European movement of political change, the second as a development of economic changes which had begun long before the years of the Industrial Revolution and are still going on. But however gradual in their development, both were revolutionary in their effects. Things were never the same again after the French Revolution—as, indeed, they were never the same again after the Russian Revolution of 1917—and Jacobinism haunted Europe after the French as did Bolshevism the world after the Russian. The London Corresponding Society, an independent working class group of 1792, and Tom Paine's *Rights of Man* of the same date, made known the exciting ideas from France, and advocated a policy of democratic political reform with a social policy closely related to it, whereby the state should use taxation to aid the helpless and the old. John Thelwall, one of the LCS leaders, made clear the democratic aim : "All ought to be consulted where all are concerned, for not less than the whole ought to decide the fate of the whole." He also gave expression to a more definitely socialistic inclination : "Let us not deceive ourselves! Property is nothing but human labour. The most inestimable of all property is the sweat of the poor man's brow; the property from which all other is derived.'

However, the French Revolution, though it had popular social pressures behind it, was in essentials a political revolution; it marked a change of government, a change, it is true, not from one dynasty to another, but from one form to another, from monarchy to republic. It marked the beginnings of democracy, of the bourgeoisie or middle class, of political liberty, of *laissez-faire* and capitalism. The Industrial Revolution, on the other hand, marked a change in the economic and social character of human existence. Taken together they profoundly affected the development of the modern world. "If," as Professor Hobsbawm has put it, "the economy of the nineteenth century world was formed mainly under the influence of the British Industrial Revolution, its politics and ideology were formed mainly by the French. Britain provided the model for its railways and factories ... but France made its revolution and gave them their ideas, to the point where a tricolour of some kind became the emblem of virtually every emerging nation, and European (or indeed world) politics between 1789 and 1917 was largely the struggle for and against the principles of

1789." All this is true. Yet at the same time the Industrial Revolution in Britain was also producing the circumstances in which a new, and different, idea would offer a new and revolutionary challenge to the existing order; this was the idea of socialism. A new idea?—rather was it an old idea which in new circumstances would acquire new meaning and new power.

The pattern of events which made up the Industrial Revolution stretches back into the past : the enclosure of the open fields and common land, improvements in cultivation and the breeding and rearing of stock, the great increase in population—from an estimated six millions in England and Wales in 1750 to nine millions in 1801, the year of the first census, and to eighteen millions by 1851, the inventions in the textile industry, the factory system, the development of mining and engineering, the application of steam power, the extension of communication and transport by roads, canals, and railways. All these things together made up the Industrial Revolution, and they transformed the face of Britain. Perhaps most important of all was the new source of power in steam; as early as 1776 the biographer Boswell visited the Soho Works of Matthew Boulton and James Watt, near Birmingham, and was much impressed to hear Boulton say : "I sell here, Sir, what all the world desires to have—Power." First used in pumping water from mines, the steam engine was developed by Watt, who converted the up and down action into a rotary movement which could be used to turn machinery. "The introduction of the rotary engine," says Professor Ashton, "was a momentous event. Coinciding as it did with that of Cort's puddling and rolling of iron, and following closely on the inventions of Arkwright and Crompton, it completely transformed the conditions of life of hundreds of thousands of men and women." In other words, here was a technical change so important that it resulted in far reaching social change. "After 1783," he continues, "when the first of the new engines was erected—

to work a hammer for John Wilkinson at Bradley—it became clear that a technological revolution was afoot in Britain. Before their patents expired in 1800, Boulton and Watt had built and put into operation about 500 engines . . . the new form of power and, no less, the new transmitting mechanisms by which this was made to do work previously done by hand and muscle, were the pivot on which industry swung into the modern age."

The old agricultural, aristocratic Britain was slowly changing into an urban and industrial Britain. In the same year that Boswell visited the Soho Works—1776, the year of the American Declaration of Independence and Adam Smith's *Wealth of Nations*, pointers both to the new world of revolutionary liberalism and capitalist *laissez faire*—Parson Woodforde was moving into the new Norfolk rectory where he would be busy writing his *Diary of a Country Parson*. For him England was still a land of countrymen leading country lives. But the Soho Works were a portent : in the coming years the country was to become less and less that of Parson Woodforde, more and more that of Boulton and Watt. Political power would pass—though very slowly—from the great landowners to the great industrialists and financiers. With steam power and steam-driven machinery and the concentration of workers in factories, great new urban areas would develop. Population shifted from the south towards the factories of the north and Midlands; new industrial areas grew up around the coal mines and iron furnaces, as in South Wales. In 1800 Manchester was the only town in Britain—other than London—which had a population exceeding 100,000; in the next 20 years, Manchester reached 150,000, and Glasgow, Edinburgh, Liverpool, and Birmingham rose above 100,000; and none of these, except Edinburgh, had been of any size or importance a century earlier. Of such social changes, some were slow and for long unnoticed, others more immediately striking, such as the Irish crossing the sea for as little as 4d a head and filling great ports like Liverpool and Glasgow, bringing with them, too, an appallingly low standard of life, and so prolonging, or even creating, slum conditions. There has been argument as to whether the Industrial Revolution improved or worsened the condition of the poor—Goldsmith's *Deserted Village* gave a somewhat idealised picture of the happiness and simplicity of country life before industrialisation. But the case of Ireland showed what could happen when population increased *without* an industrial revolution. In the 1840s she lost about one-fifth of her population by emigration, starvation, and disease. In Britain, on the other hand, the Industrial Revolution (even though for many years from 1793 to 1815, the country was at war) made it possible to employ, to feed, to clothe, and to house a population greater than in any preceding age—and, ultimately, at a higher standard of life. The problems that came, hand in hand with economic and social change, were, not unnaturally, immense : a demand for a share in power for the new industrial classes, the problem of poverty on a large scale, slums and the absence of sanitation in the new towns, epidemics and disease—cholera, typhoid, smallpox, problems, too, of religion and education.

Amid all this, one striking feature is the emergence of new social classes, the middle class, and also the working classes, which when thought of as united are termed working class or proletariat. Long before Marx had written, the economist Sismondi, writing in 1819, pointed out that "the fundamental change which has taken place in society, amid this universal struggle created by competition, is the introduction of the 'proletary' ". More dramatic was a French writer's description of the position a few years later : "Every manufacturer lives in his factory like the colonial planters in the midst of their slaves, one against a hundred ... the barbarians who menace society are neither in the Caucasus nor in the steppes of Tartary; they are in the suburbs of our industrial cities ... the middle class must clearly recognise

the nature of the situation; it must know where it stands."
Disraeli's novel *Sybil* of 1845 makes the same point very
clearly when a character refers to the queen ruling over two
nations—"Two nations; between whom there is no inter-
course and no sympathy; who are as ignorant of each other's
habits, thoughts and feelings, as if they were dwellers in
different zones, or inhabitants of different planets; who are
formed by a different breeding, are fed by a different food,
are ordered by different manners, and are not governed by
the same laws— the Rich and the Poor." The workers on
their part might well feel overwhelmed and crushed by the
new power of machinery and the new discipline of the
factory. "A steam engine," it was said, "in the hands of an
interested or avaricious master is a relentless power to
which old and young are equally bound to submit." Arguments drawn from negro slavery were also used. Those who
had interests in the plantations would argue that their slaves
were better off than the factory workers in England. The
workers at home might maintain that, while the negroes
were slaves in name, they were slaves in reality. Robert
Owen also thought the cotton workers worse off than the
slaves he had seen in the West Indies. Common sufferings
and common interests drew the workers together. But the
sufferings were not as great nor the common interests as
common, or as clearly perceived, as Sismondi, or the French
bourgeois, or Disraeli might have feared; in practice the
working classes did not present a common front to the
masters as, in theory, they might have done. Nevertheless
the emergence of the new class was a characteristic and most
important feature of the industrial age. It was during the
period of the Industrial Revolution that the very words we
employ so frequently in discussing modern economic and
social problems came into general use—as Professor Hobsbawm points out—such words as "working class", "middle
class", "industry", "factory", "capitalism", "socialism".

The workers' response to the threat and challenge of the

new industrialism—the pace of which varied from industry to industry—was various and not of one kind. For the workers too, like other members of the new industrial society, were human beings, and not mere "economic" men. They did not, therefore, they could not, present a common front, as, when looked on merely as economic men, they theoretically might have done. They were not simply concerned with their conditions of life : some were, doubtless, too much exhausted by hardship to be concerned at all, others might incline to other interests, political, religious, family or local. Their response covered the whole possible range of protest : from blank indifference, through unthinking violence, to planned and constructive organisation. And the more thoughtful the organisation, the later it was likely to come— for thinking takes time, and at first few, if any, whether statesmen, or busy and confident employers, or workmen largely without suitable educational facilities, understood the real nature of the developments going on around them and what they would lead to. Few, if any, could see even a few years ahead, any more than we in the 1930s could foresee the coming of full employment, the affluent society, the population explosion, the expansion of universities, and the growth of air travel and the decline of the railways.

Riots and disturbances were, of course, nothing new, especially among the London apprentices and journeymen. Rioting might well be a form of collective bargaining. But now workers could find some concrete enemy to fight, namely the machinery which appeared to rob them of their jobs. Here, however, was a clear example of the workers being divided in their interests; the same machinery which took work from some, gave it to others. Those who broke the machines were not the factory workers in general, but rather those who were employed in the older domestic system, for example, the frame-work knitters of Nottingham and the hand-loom weavers of Lancashire. Thus the Luddites—so called after the name of some unidentified leader in Nottinghamshire or Leicestershire—broke machinery, in 1811, 1812, and 1816. There had, indeed, been similar disturbances earlier, as when in 1792 hand-loom weavers in Manchester destroyed a factory using Cartwright's power-loom. There were farm labourers' revolts in the rural counties of southern England in the winter of 1830-31 against threshing machines. As a result three men were hanged. Other small popular disturbances occurred in London at Spa Fields and in Scotland (Bonnymuir), but the most famous is the so-called Peterloo massacre, at St Peter's Fields, Manchester, in 1819. An apparently peaceful but large crowd demonstrating in favour of parliamentary reform and the repeal of the Corn Laws was, on the order of the probably over-anxious local magistrates, broken up by cavalry. In the resulting disorder, eleven people were killed, and hundreds injured. Peterloo was long remembered with horror and disgust. It was an outstanding example—and therefore remembered—of the occasional breakdown of British forbearance and tolerance.

For violence was not typical. Much more characteristic of the working class movement was the workers' efforts to protect themselves by organisation. And this was not entirely new. The Webbs in their classic *History of Trade Unionism* denied the existence of a link between the unions and the old Craft Guilds, but more recently it has been suggested that some of the small unions did in fact show some of the older characteristics. The craftsmen, both small master and journeyman, had sometimes a strong attachment to their trade and a sense of the dignity of their craft; processions, festivals, bands were backward-looking to tradition. The union, sometimes appearing to the outside world as a friendly society, existed to safeguard the interests of its members; sometimes it was a continuous association, but sometimes a union might be formed to deal with some immediate problem or dispute; sometimes, too, workers might be organised to resist the setting up of machinery in certain trades or the admission of new men. Friendly Societies developed as a means of mutual protection against illness and old age, and membership increased greatly between 1800 and 1850. The authorities regarded trade unions with suspicion, and in fact, there were already in existence a number of laws against them. Of such laws the Combination Acts of 1799-1800 were the best known and were directed towards suppressing unions altogether. The number of prosecutions was small, however, and the authorities seem in general to have sought conciliation rather than a rigid enforcement of the law. Certainly unionism was not stamped out, although it may sometimes have been driven underground; workers could combine informally, but dispense with meeting in public and the keeping of written records. In 1824 the Combination Acts were repealed, and the unions found a little more freedom of action. In the following years there were renewed attempts—inspired partly by the ideas of Robert Owen—to build up stronger organisations on a basis of working class solidarity. Perhaps the chief working class leader of the time was John Doherty. Coming as a boy from Ireland to Manchester, he worked in the cotton mills and led a great strike in 1829. Realising that the working classes must be organised, he formed in 1830 a National Association for the Protection of Labour; he thought, too, that the working classes should organise their own education; and, accepting as inevitable the coming of the new machinery, he argued that it must be brought under the control of the working classes themselves. Other schemes of union were going on at the same time, among the builders, woollen workers, miners, and the various workers' groups in London. This wave of activity reached its peak in 1834 with the Grand National Consolidated Trades Union, to which Owen gave his support. Its object was, at one go, to bring the system of capitalism to an end and put in its place a universal co-operation under the control of the workers. But the whole scheme petered out in the following

* *

year. This was partly because it became involved in sectional, local strikes, when employers made jobs depend on signing the "document" which forswore union membership, partly due to weaknesses in its own position and organisation. At the same time the savage sentence of transportation on six Dorchester labourers, who had formed a union but unwittingly broken a law of 1797 against illegal oaths, also marked the downfall of the unions. Indeed, the fact was that the unions had tried to do too much; they had tried to run before they could walk. Many years of painstaking organisation were necessary before they could be strong, and even then they would have, to achieve success, to aim at more limited objectives.

Another form which the workers' movement for self-help took—often aided by philanthropists from other social classes—was co-operation. There were producers' co-operatives and consumers' co-operatives. The idea was that a group of workers should produce and sell goods without a capitalist employer and so keep the profits in their own hands. In different parts of the country societies or stores were set up; they might well have the immediate object of alleviating unemployment and safeguarding the consumer against high prices. They offered a practical solution—to protect groups of workers against economic change. The idealism of the Owenites gave a more general character to the movement—as in the case of the trade unions, local efforts led on to an attempt to create a movement on national lines. Supporters of co-operation looked forward to the setting up of villages or communities run on co-operative or socialist lines; the profits from a co-operative store could be put towards the formation of a capital fund to found the community. Sometimes a co-operative workshop would be set up, and its products sold in a co-operative exchange or bazaar in London or some other town. But—again as in the case of the trade unions—little came of all this at the time. It was only later, in 1844, that the Toad Lane store was opened in Rochdale, from which the modern co-operative movement is generally said to have grown—yet Toad Lane was not really different in character from the earlier societies. Its importance was that it managed to survive.

There were, too, other movements and interests which might attract members of the working classes, such as the struggle for parliamentary reform (led by such men as Harry Hunt, William Cobbett, and Francis Place—Radicals, but not socialists) and for free trade, the repeal of the Corn Laws and cheap food. The Reform Act of 1832 in effect gave the vote to the middle class and left out the working classes; working class organisations had indeed long supported an extension of the franchise, and the Bristol riots illustrated the mob element in the movement. Workers might turn also to religion or to education. The Methodist and other Nonconformist chapels offered a meeting place and also a share in control and organisation, giving experience which could be useful in the wider social struggle. And religion and political and economic movements were closely interconnected, as in the Owenite and Chartist churches. Most working class leaders believed in education. Mechanics Institutes could help the intelligent and persevering artisan, and the Chartist leaders, William Lovett and Thomas Cooper, both overcame great difficulties in their hard working lives to educate themselves. As Lovett put it: "How can a corrupt government stand against an enlightened people?"

The Chartist movement, best known of all the working class movements of this time, stood mainly for political aims —the Charter asked for universal manhood suffrage. But beyond this the Chartists looked to the vote as a means to economic improvement; their demands gained strength from the general dissatisfaction with the economic system and the need for a working class movement to maintain and support working people in their struggle against the powerful forces of the established order, the government, an unrepresentative parliament, and the employers.

Chartism had its left wing, men like Bronterre O'Brien, George Julian Harney, and Ernest Jones, who went beyond the Charter to a policy of socialism. O'Brien published in 1836 his translation of Buonarotti's history of the Babeuf communist conspiracy in the Paris of 1796, and thought that the working class must destroy the power of the middle class in order to achieve a social revolution. For Harney Chartism was "The Charter and something more", as he put it in his periodical *Red Republican* in 1850; they had "progressed . . . to the idea of a social revolution", and it was Harney's *Red Republican* which published, in the same year, the first English translation of the *Communist Manifesto* of Marx and Engels. Harney looked for "not any patching and cobbling of the present system . . . but the annihilation of that system". Ernest Jones, a man well off and of good position, a barrister by profession, became a convinced socialist. He suffered two years of prison—under cruel conditions—for his Chartist activities in 1848, and his views went far beyond the Charter. He was much influenced by Marx and the idea of the class war, and looked for the replacement of the capitalist system by socialism. When Jones died in 1869 Engels wrote to Marx that "he was the only educated Englishman among the politicians who was, at bottom, entirely on our side". Thus the Chartists established links with Karl Marx, the prophet of revolutionary socialism.

The Chartist groups in different parts of the country were, like the unions and co-operative societies, not closely organised and disciplined. Some were for moral force and persuasion, others seemed to favour physical force, like Fergus O'Connor, the proprietor of the popular workers' paper, the *Northern Star*. The Charter was launched in 1838 by Lovett and others, and in the following year a convention was called in London and it presented to parliament a mammoth petition. The petition was rejected, and the extremists diverted Chartist energies into direct action—there were mob attacks on policemen in Birmingham, there was trouble in Newcastle, in Llanidloes, and in Monmouthshire the miners lost a number killed in an attempt to free an imprisoned leader in Newport. The Chartists discussed proposals for a general strike or "Sacred Month", but little came of it. In 1842 a second petition was presented and rejected. Chartism appeared for the last time in 1848, the year of revolutions in Continental Europe. But the Chartist march on Westminster in support of their petition was easily stopped by the authorities. It was the last great working class demonstration for many years to come, and Chartism slowly petered out.

Amid these many working class movements of resistance to the hardships and oppressions of the Industrial Revolution there is to be found also a considerable reaction to and criticism of the economic theory of capitalism, accompanied by proposals for reform of various kinds; some critics accepted, in the main, the competitive system of free enterprise but advocated strong trade unions to struggle for the workers' share; others proposed currency reform, an expansion of bank credit to encourage production and employment; others, yet again, put forward some kind of socialist solution, usually some organisation of the workers themselves to create a productive community rather than the organisation of production by the state in the sense of modern socialism. A considerable body of writing exists by a considerable number of men; Spence, Godwin, Hodgskin, and Thompson may be taken as examples. Thomas Spence (1750-1814) advocated communal ownership of land by local communes; after his death his followers intended a coup, on the lines of Babeuf—the Cato Street Conspiracy of 1820, when Thistlewood and a group of Spenceans planned to murder the cabinet and seize power. William Godwin (1756-1836), father-in-law of Shelley, was a believer in the ideal freedom of the eighteenth century thinkers; men required no government, but could rely on good sense, they should cultivate the land and share the products of their combined labour. Thomas Hodgskin (1783-1869) and William Thompson (1783-1833) were strong critics of Ricardo's economics. Ricardo for them stood for the capitalist economics of the time. He had pointed to labour as the source of value. This his working-class critics willingly accepted, and went on to argue that, in that case, labour should receive the full amount of its product and not be forced down, by competition, to a subsistence level. What they too easily left out of account was the managing ability, enterprise, and energy of the employer—this might well be considered by the economists as a part of labour, and puts the facile labour theory of value in a different light. Thompson thought that the solution would lie in a complete system of community living, and in this he was more clearly socialist than many other such writers. To what did all these theories amount? It would, perhaps, be unfair to regard Spence as typical. Yet, in one way, one feels the truth of the dry pointed way in which Sir John Clapham picked out the words in which Radical, Francis Place, described Spence whom he knew well—"not more than five feet high ... unpractical in the ways of the world to an extent hardly imaginable".

2. Robert Owen and Socialism

IF SPENCE WAS "unpractical in the ways of the world", the outstanding thing about Robert Owen (1771-1858) was that he was exceedingly practical in everyday affairs and brilliantly successful in business. He is an example—and a striking one—of the self-made man, the characteristic figure of the industrial age. At the same time he is the most famous figure in the early history of British socialism; his name has never been forgotten, and Attlee went back beyond Marx to Robert Owen as the founder of the movement in this country. In his own day his name was known all over Europe and America, and the great ones of the earth made his acquaintance as well as the thinkers and the leaders of the working classes; a copy of his *New View of Society* reached Napoleon at Elba and, we are told, the fallen emperor read it and asked for information about the author. Today some account of the life and ideas of Owen finds a place in every social and economic history; his works have been translated into numerous languages and studied in many lands—and that not only in the west, for one of the most complete bibliographies of his works has been compiled in Japan. And Owen is significant because, though a great industrialist himself, he could not accept the prevalent competitive economics of his fellow industrialists; he considered that the new production forces must be subjected to social control for the common good. Against competition he put his new principle of co-operation. He was the pioneer of British socialism.

Robert Owen was born in 1771 in Newtown, Montgomeryshire, and stands in line with the other great political and social reformers who have come from Wales to England —Oliver Cromwell (whose ancestors the Williams family came from Llanishen, near Cardiff), Lloyd George, and Aneurin Bevan. When Owen was born the Industrial Revolution was only just beginning, and in the quiet countryside around the little market town he grew up in conditions quite unaffected by the industrial changes which were getting under way in distant parts of Britain. His father was a tradesman—saddler and ironmonger and also the local postmaster. The young Robert went to a village school, was studious but also popular and keen on games with his fellows, and by seven had learnt apparently all the teachers could give of reading, writing, and arithmetic, for he was made usher or assistant teacher. At nine he left school and worked in a shop next door to his home. His boyhood was happy: no serious problem worried him in the mid-Wales country life with its rough social equality among the farmers and tradesmen. He was on good terms with all, and the vicar, doctor, and lawyer lent him books; he read, in addition to literature, travel books and history. At ten he left home to seek his fortune, taking the coach from Shrewsbury to London, where he had a brother already established in business. Through friends of his father in London, Robert was apprenticed to a substantial draper in Stamford, Lincolnshire. He did well, read widely in his spare time, improved his manners in contact with the nobility and gentry who patronised the business, and was pressed to stay on at the end of his apprenticeship. But he went on to another drapery in London, and then to a wholesale and retail business in Manchester. So he acquired a good knowledge of various kinds of drapery business, and he became a judge of fabrics.

Now, at eighteen, Owen started his great adventure: with a little capital borrowed from his brother, he began, in partnership with a mechanic, to manufacture machines for cotton spinning: then he set up on his own and rented a new factory building to spin and sell cotton thread; next he took on the job of manager of a large spinning mill with 500 employees. His success was astonishing; he became known as one of the finest cotton spinners and various offers came his way, resulting in his joining as a partner in a powerful firm, the Chorlton Twist Company. Owen now began to make business visits, including trips to Scotland, which led, on Owen's initiative, to the Chorlton Twist Company buying the New Lanark Mills (cotton spinning) from David Dale, a leading Scottish industrialist and banker, and to Owen marrying Dale's daughter. And so, at the beginning of 1800, while one of the partners remained in Manchester to run the business there, Owen was established as the resident managing director at the New Lanark Mills, which were to be indelibly linked with his name. For the next twenty-five years he was in control, although his plans for improvements led to trouble with the partners, and on two occasions Owen had to form new partnerships (on the second occasion including Jeremy Bentham) and buy out the old partners. Owen made a tremendous success of the mills—profits were large, and he won the love of his work-people; he gradually got rid of drunkenness and thieving; he built up a co-operative but paternalistic community under his own control. A few years later he was employing about 2,000 workers. There were company shops buying in bulk, and providing the best quality at lower prices; he enlarged the workers' houses and built new ones; he arranged for street cleaning and refuse collection; he had health visitors to see that homes were clean inside. As time went on he was able to introduce further improvements. In 1816 he reduced the hours of work to ten and a half, and provided free medical attention, a sick club, and a savings bank. He established schools for the children, including infant schools, with drill and marching exercises, singing and dancing, as well as elementary instruction in an atmosphere of freedom, and without corporal punishment. In the evenings there was education for adults. The schools were visited by many famous people, and Owen became widely known as a philanthropist.

Meanwhile Owen's ideas and plans were taking clearer shape, and developing towards a national significance. Education, for him, was fundamental—"The best governed state will be that which shall possess the best national system of education"—and he thought particularly of training the character. "Yet (will future ages credit the fact?)," he went on, "to this day the British Government is without any national system of training and education, even for its millions of poor and uninstructed. The formation of the mind and habits of its subjects is permitted to go on at random, often in the hands of those who are the most incompetent in the empire; and the result is the gross ignorance and disunion which now everywhere abound!" To put matters right he says, "an Act should be passed for the instruction of all the poor and labouring classes in the three kingdoms". These ideas Owen set out in his *New View of Society* (or *Essays on the Principle of the Formation of the Human Character*), published in 1814, when he was at the height of his powers, and known and admired for his success at New Lanark. In this book of essays he developed the view—which he held to be fundamental—that environment is paramount in forming men's characters and ideas. He held that all previous ages and social systems had been in error in holding each individual man responsible for his own sentiments and habits, and consequently meriting reward for some and punishment for others. But now, he wrote, it is becoming evident "that the character of man is, without a single exception, always formed for him; that it may be, and is, chiefly created by his predecessors; that they give him, or may give him, his ideas and habits, which are the powers that govern and direct his conduct. Man, therefore, never did, nor is it possible he ever can, form his own character." Hence, then, the importance of a proper environment, of early training and education, starting with the child or even the infant—such a process he regarded as the necessary preparation for socialism or any new social order.

But the socialist character of Owen's thinking was not at first apparent. During 1813-14 he spent some time in London and was busy with arrangements for his book and for his new business partnership, of which Bentham became a member. He met many other leading figures of the time, Godwin, Francis Place, James Mill, Malthus, Wilberforce. He met also, members of the ruling classes, including the prime minister, Lord Liverpool, the home secretary, Lord Sidmouth, and the archbishop of Canterbury, to whom at

Lambeth he read two of his essays. "I wished them to see and know all I was doing and intended to do," Owen wrote later in his autobiography, "being conscious that all parties from the highest to the lowest would be benefited by my views of society." It is, perhaps, difficult to picture the leaders of what has generally been thought of as a reactionary government receiving Owen, but he was evidently a man with great charm of personality and he was accepted, at this time, as one who had achieved great practical success and might have valuable suggestions to make. His paternalism was welcome to the Tories, and if he could deal with poverty the burden of the poor rate would be reduced. Copies of Owen's book were sent, with Sidmouth's help, to the leading governments of Europe and America, to the universities, and to the English and Irish bishops, and, through the American Ambassador, to the governors of the States in the USA. In the next year or two Owen was busy with a more limited— but more immediate—project. He wished to have a factory law to protect children and others employed in cotton, wool, and other textile mills. He failed to gain the support of Scottish employers, and came again to London to appeal to the government and to parliament. He carried on a considerable campaign, finally gaining the help of the first Sir Robert Peel (who had carried the Health and Morals of Apprentices Act of 1802). Now a long process of consultation, enquiry, and parliamentary committees followed, and the bill was not passed until 1819, and then so much emasculated, that Owen was thoroughly disappointed. Nevertheless the Act did establish the state's right to interfere to safeguard ordinary labour—for the earlier Act of 1802 had applied only to "apprentice" children.

Long before the passing of the Factory Act Owen had been actively involved in moves to deal with the distress following peace in 1815. Peace brought to an end the government's demand for all kinds of supplies for the army, led to a fall in prices and consequently in employment, and

the soldiers returning from the war added to the unemployment. A meeting in 1816 of notable people under the chairmanship of the Duke of York elected a committee, of which
Owen was a member, to seek remedies, and Owen was asked
to prepare for the committee his views on the causes of the
distress and what could be done. His *Report to the Committee of the Association for the Relief of the Manufacturing
and Labouring Poor* (1817) shows him moving from the
position of factory and educational reformer towards that
of socialist pioneer. He saw the immediate cause of the
trouble in the depreciation of human labour, brought about
by the introduction of machinery and the ending of wartime
demand. At the same time the new machinery gave society
a vastly increased power of production. Owen maintained
that one of three things must come about :

1. The use of machinery must be greatly diminished;
2. Millions of human beings must starve, machinery
   taking their place;
3. Some useful occupation must be found for the poor
   and unemployed, and machinery must not be allowed
   to take the place of their labour.

The first and second were unthinkable, but the third
possibility suggested a line of action; in effect, Owen was
calling on society, or the State, to provide employment for
the distressed, and this was a step towards socialism. Owen
produced a plan for the foundation of "villages of mutual
co-operation". In proposing these Owen had in mind his
model economic community at New Lanark, but the new
villages of co-operation would be self-supporting, or nearly
self-supporting, agricultural communities. Perhaps Owen
was looking back to the peaceful life of his boyhood in
Montgomery. The French socialist, Fourier, put forward at
the same time a scheme for an agricultural community. Owen
thought the authorities—the government, or districts,

or even individuals—should set up a capital sum, to provide a sufficient tract of land for each village; to work the land villages should be built, each to house about 1,200 men, women, and children. In addition to farming, the village would have its own workshops to produce what was wanted. The village should buy little from outside, and would only sell any surplus it might have; villages could make exchanges with each other. Inside the villages there should be a strong community organisation; each family would have its own accommodation, but there would be communal cooking and meals, and common recreation and reading rooms. Only infants would sleep at home with the parents; the other children would sleep in a boarding house. There would be a school for the infants, and one for the older children. The buildings were to take the shape of a quadrangle—Owen's "parallelogram" as it came to be called—and were to be surrounded by gardens. Owen calculated that the villages would be self-supporting, would be able to pay interest on the capital used to start them going, and in time would pay back the capital sum itself. They would, too, replace the existing poor law; and whereas poor relief was unproductive and allowed the workers to deteriorate, villages of co-operation would employ the workers to the full and give them renewed spirit. But the committee felt unable to handle Owen's report; it was referred to a parliamentary committee which had been set up to consider the poor law, and this committee set it aside.

Owen next turned to the public, through the press, through pamphlets, and through public meetings. At one of these meetings he attacked religion, an action, at the least, inexpedient. What he was attacking really was the element of myth and untruth in all religions—later on in life he could speak of "the Supreme Power of Creation" and "the good and superior Spirit". He feared that religious differences would be carried into his villages of co-operation and that intolerance might destroy them. He made this attack after deliberation, and he himself afterwards saw his action as a turning point in his career. It seems a strange and unnecessary action for Owen to have taken—for he was an eminently religious man in his ideals and his conduct, if not in his beliefs (he could not reconcile the existence of so many religions, and even of so many Christian sects). If he really thought—as he suggests in his autobiography—that he could at one go rid mankind of ignorance and superstition, then he was losing his grip on reality. His attack aroused opposition to his cause, for now those who opposed him would add the charge of atheism. This did him no good, but there was, perhaps, another reason for his plan failing to gain acceptance. The government was becoming seriously alarmed by the distress of the times, by the popular disturbances, and by reports of plots for the overthrow of all authority. This led authority to look to repression rather than social schemes as suggested by Owen, and repression culminated, after Peterloo, in the Six Acts (restricting public meetings, and curtailing popular newspapers by heavy taxation). Owen, certainly at this time, was no revolutionary; he had appealed to the ruling classes, and he mixed with the wealthy and well-to-do; he did not believe in the Radicals' proposals for parliamentary reform, thinking that men must first be improved by education and social conditions—nevertheless Owen's constructive proposals did not gain the necessary support. Even a committee presided over by the Duke of Kent (Queen Victoria's father), who was a strong friend, failed to enlist support; an appeal in 1819 for funds by private subscription to set up one village on Owenite lines was unsuccessful, and even the committee was dissolved.

In Scotland Owen expounded his views once more. A Committee of leading gentlemen in the county of Lanark asked him to help in finding means for relieving distress. He set out his views in what is his fullest and most mature statement—his *Report to the County of Lanark* (1820). This is the best and clearest expression of Owenism or Owenite socialism. Owen saw his task as finding a remedy for "the general want of employment", but did not think employment could be found through trade, manufacture, or even agriculture, unless the government would take certain measures to make possible the distribution of the vastly increased wealth that machinery was making available. "Manual labour," he says, "properly directed, is the source of all wealth and of national prosperity." In this, in making labour the source of wealth, he was at one with many socialist writers, though he guarded himself, it will be noted, by the phrase "properly directed". And a similar safeguard is observed again when he says: "The natural standard of value is, in principle, human labour; or combined manual and mental powers of men called into action". Such qualifications allow for the part of the employer, manager, or capitalist in the productive process, and it is perhaps surprising that Owen does not make more of this. He maintains that labour—presumably "properly directed"—can always produce a surplus over what is necessary to maintain the labourer in decent comfort. The problem is not to produce enough, but to distribute what, with the new industrial power, can be easily produced. Owen saw this clearly enough, but he could not foresee how difficult this problem was and how long it would take to solve it—how often one heard Owen's point made again in the 1930s when huge surpluses of materials and goods existed alongside world-wide unemployment. Owen saw, too, that the low wages of the workers meant that purchasing power was not enough to buy the goods the workers produced. "The markets of the world," he says, "are created solely by the remuneration allowed for the industry of the working classes, and those markets are more or less extended and profitable in proportion as those classes are well or ill remunerated for their labour. But the existing arrangements of society will not permit the labourer to be remunerated for his industry, and in consequence all markets fail." He saw that gold had its weakness as a standard of value; the return to the gold standard in 1819 (as again in 1925!) depressed prices. Perhaps one could say that there was not enough money to enable consumers to buy the vastly increased output of the new industry. He suggested creating a new standard of value and basis for credit in order "to let prosperity loose on the country", as he put it; this new standard would be based on human labour. The value of the labour in every article produced could be calculated, and a fairer system of exchange replace the existing system of wages and market bargaining. As well as benefiting the labourer, this would also get rid of the risks the landowner and capitalist faced due to the fluctuations of the market.

Next Owen went on to expound once more his idea of villages of co-operation based on agriculture but with the necessary manufactures also. He saw that they must be virtually self-supporting, for if the workers produced more goods for the ordinary markets there would be over-production and a still further depression of prices. The villages took on now an even more socialistic or communist character. They must be "founded on the principle of united labour, expenditure and property, and equal privileges". And again : "There will be no desire or motive for individual accumulation of wealth." At the same time Owen attacked specialisation and division of labour, feeling that this reduced the worker to a mechanism and robbed him of his dignity (again, like Fourier) "minute division of labour and division of interests are only other terms for poverty, ignorance, waste of every kind, universal opposition throughout society, crime, misery, and great bodily and mental imbecility". He might even have had in mind to answer Adam Smith's admiration for the division of labour as demonstrated in a pin factory : "One man draws out the wire, another straightens it . . . a fourth points it . . . " By this means thousands of pins a day were produced whereas one man working singly could have produced a few only. The economist thought first of the amount of the product; the socialist thought rather of the effect on the worker. For in his villages, Owen argued, where every child would get an all-round education and each adult worker combine agricultural with manufacturing work, "instead of the unhealthy pointer of a pin,—header of a nail, —piecer of a thread,—or clod-hopper, senselessly gazing at the soil . . . there would spring up a working class full of activity and useful knowledge". As for the government of his villages, it would depend upon who formed them. If formed by a landowner or capitalist, the villages would be run under their direction; if set up by co-operative enterprise, they should be self-governing. The County of Lanark committee were impressed by Owen's proposals, but they wished to send criminals to join the village they proposed. To this Owen objected, and the scheme lapsed. Owen, however, was ever active, and by now he had other schemes in mind.

A very wealthy man and active philanthropist, Owen had become an international figure; his energy was immense. He had toured the Continent : he was made much of in Paris, in Switzerland he visited the schools of Oberlin, Pestalozzi, and Fellenberg, he met German politicians, and at the Great Power Conference of Aix-la-Chapelle his two *Memorials on behalf of the Working Classes* were laid before the conference by Lord Castlereagh. Now, in 1822, he had a great reception in Ireland. In 1824 he went to America to inspect the property of the Rappites in Indiana. This—now up for sale because its owners were moving to a new site—was a colony of a religious kind, led by George Rapp, an emigrant from Germany. Owen bought the whole estate and called it New Harmony; here, in the New World, he could make a real attempt to put his theories into practice. In 1825 he gave up his managerial position at New Lanark, and three years later sold his share in the business. From 1824 to 1829 New Harmony was his main preoccupation.

The experiment started well. There was in existence already a village of cottages, a silk mill, and a woollen mill.

Owen lectured in Washington—before the President and many leading public men—and elsewhere, and he invited settlers to come to join his settlement. They did—so many, that there was some confusion at first. But gradually order was established, and a constitution based on equality worked out, allowing for an elected governing council. Soon, however, discords arose, over the elective practice which some disliked, and over religion; there were splits, and reunions. By 1828 Owen could see that the experiment was failing, and he wound up the community. He leased or sold the land; his four sons remained there, and became American citizens. The winding-up involved Owen in very heavy financial loss; he did not lose faith in the community principle, however, but blamed the failure on insufficient preparation. "I tried here a new course for which I was induced to hope that fifty years of political liberty had prepared the American population.... I supplied land, houses, and the use of much capital" but "experience proved that the attempt was premature to unite a number of strangers not previously educated for the purpose, who should carry on extensive operations for their common interest, and live together as a common family." What happened was that those who had taken land on lease began to work for their own gain, as did also the storekeepers. And it became evident that "families trained in the individual system ... have not acquired those moral qualities of forbearance and charity for each other ... without which communities cannot exist." Man's character, indeed, is formed for him—Owen's own principle! Owen was himself directly connected with another community in 1839—this was Harmony Hall, or Queenwood, in Hampshire—and his followers set up Orbiston in Scotland and Ralahine in Ireland. None of these communities had any lasting success.

When Owen came back to England in 1829 he came into contact with the growing self-consciousness of the working class. Trade unions and co-operative societies had been much

influenced by Owenism. And Owen himself, having failed
to win over the ruling classes to his ideas, was more inclined
to see in working class organisations the means of realising
his hopes and ideals. The co-operative societies were particularly active, co-operative congresses were held, and two
exchange bazaars were set up. In 1832 Owen set up his own
exchange in London—the National Equitable Labour
Exchange, with a new currency of Labour Notes based on
labour power. Goods came to the exchange in considerable
quantities from societies of co-operative producers—carpen-
ters, bootmakers, tailors; those who brought goods also made
purchases, as did the general public. But by 1834 trade was
falling off, and this exchange—as also one in Birmingham—
was wound up.

Meanwhile, by the middle of 1833 Owen came to be
virtually leader of the working class movement. There was
at this time in trade unionism and co-operation something of
the spirit of a religious revival. Owen seemed himself to
be inspired with the thought of the coming millennium; he
moved up and down the country, tireless in his lectures and
talks with working class leaders. The new age was dawning,
the age of Co-operation which would replace the old system.
"You may accomplish this change," he told the Operative
Builders' Union, "for the whole population of the British
Empire in less than five years, and essentially ameliorate
the condition of the producing class throughout Great
Britain and Ireland in less than five months." Owen was
looking now, not to trade union action to reform one
industry, not to a village of co-operation here or there,
but to a reorganisation of society as a whole, in short, to
a New Moral World. Meetings and congresses went on, in
many parts of the country, and in London in February,
1834, a congress of delegates formed the Grand National
Consolidated Trades Union. Modern research suggests that
the national name was misleading, and that the movement
was largely based on London. And it is not clear what the

relation was of some existing large national unions—Builders, Spinners, Potters, and Clothiers—to the new organisation. The unions had practical aims—better wages and hours; Owen and his followers aimed rather at moral regeneration. As we saw in Chapter 1, the Consolidated movement soon petered out : local unions expended their efforts on local strikes before the Consolidated Union was ready for a general strike (aimed at securing an eight hour day and, perhaps, a peaceful revolution); the authorities struck at the Tolpuddle labourers; and Owen quarrelled with his ablest lieutenants in the movement, James Morrison, editor of *Pioneer*, the paper of the Consolidated Union, and J. E. Smith, editor of *Crisis*, the journal of Owenite co-operators. Smith alleged that Owen was too full of himself and wanted to be dictator of the movement. The quarrel was partly over religion—once again Owen's bugbear—partly over the methods of securing revolutionary change. Owen was prepared to use the general strike but he insisted on its being peaceful : "All the individuals now living are the suffering victims of this accursed system, and all are objects of pity : you will, therefore, effect this great and glorious revolution without, if possible . . . bloodshed, violence, or evil of any kind, merely by an overwhelming moral influence, which influence individuals and nations will speedily perceive the uselessness and folly of attempting to resist." Owen soon realised that the immediate objective, the general strike, was not practicable; he persuaded a congress of Owenite societies to set up instead a British and Foreign Consolidated Association of Industry, Humanity, and Knowledge to bring about the reconciliation of employers and workers, and he replaced *Crisis* by a publication to be known as the *New Moral World*. The Consolidated Union, apparently, went on for a few months without Owen, but the great concerted effort of trade unionism was over. Not that trade union activity ceased. The energies of the working classes turned to the movement for factory reform, the anti-poor law movement, and a little later to Chartism; Owen himself, still with many Owenite societies behind him, went on almost as if nothing had happened, but he turned more to moral persuasion for moral reformation, to social or ethical religion of a rational kind, and, eventually, to spiritualism. His wonderful energy and courage, his lectures in this country and America, his interest in mankind went on to the end. On a visit to the place of his birth in 1858, he died and was buried, near his parents, in the churchyard at Newtown.

Owen saw very clearly the essential weakness in the capitalism of his time, as he analysed it in his *Report to the County of Lanark*—"in the midst of the most ample means to create wealth, all are in poverty, or in imminent danger from the effects of poverty upon others". "Poverty in the midst of plenty"—how often was that cry heard during the world depression of the 1930s! And like the critics of capitalism in the 1930s, Owen, too, saw the system as at fault. It is, he wrote, "a received opinion among theorists in political economy, that man can provide better for himself, and more advantageously for the public, when . . . in competition with his fellows". This principle, he continued, "is considered, by the most celebrated political economists, to be the corner-stone to the social system". Yet it produces all the evils of social life. Over against it Owen put "the wonderful effects which combination and union can produce". Owen looked forward to the world being organised on the principles of "the new born Social Science" (he does not use the word socialism). "This science," he wrote at the very end of his life, "will be soon found to be the science of sciences, through a knowledge of which the population of the world will be permanently well-fed, clothed, lodged, trained, educated, employed, recreated, and governed, by being placed within circumstances or surroundings scientifically devised and executed to produce with the certainty of a law of nature all these results."

It should be remembered, however, how much of all this depended on Owen himself. His religious background—though he attacked accepted religion—and his serious but optimistic character explained his millennial characteristic: he was always expecting the new age to begin. Where he succeeded, and succeeded brilliantly, at New Lanark, he was personally in charge—his was paternal socialism; where every Tom, Dick, and Harry could put obstacles in his way, as at New Harmony, he failed. As with so many successful men, there was also an element of good luck in his success in business. At New Lanark it was his personality (rather than, as he supposed, his principle of character formation by environment) that won over his work people and established them as a model community. He was, in every sense, a self-made man. And his belief in education—why did he attach so much importance to education, when he himself had got on so well with so little? Clearly it was not education as ordinarily understood, not the classical education of the grammar schools and the Oxford and Cambridge of his day. By education, he meant surrounding the young with the kind of environment he, Owen, thought right for them. Yet when all is said and done, he had an incomparable vision of what a socialist commonwealth, a New Moral World, might be. No other socialist thinker in Britain, for many years to come, would be so influential.

3. Other Socialistic Voices

OWEN IS THE giant in the early history of British socialism, but there were other figures. Quite apart from working class writers on economics, there was during the nineteenth century a steady undercurrent of criticism of the capitalist system and its competitive economies. The "nest of singing birds" at the Lakes—especially Coleridge—would have none of it. Carlyle characterised economics as "the dismal science". The Oxford Movement opposed liberalism in theology and in politics, but also in the economic sphere. Newman contrasted the Christian view of wealth with the views prevalent in his day, and pointed out the difference between wealth and moral welfare. Ruskin, Comte, John Stuart Mill, Darwin are all among those who to some degree were critical of the economic system existing in their time, or whose ideas led to men looking at society in a new way. Although Conservatives such as Pitt, Huskisson, and Peel accepted the new industrialisation, older Tory opinion, hating the brash newly-rich manufacturers and their new world of machinery, factories, and class division, looked back to a supposed older and better world, as it was pictured by Lord John Manners:

> Each knew his place—king, peasant, peer, or priest,
> The greatest owned connection with the least;
> From rank to rank the generous feeling ran,
> And linked society as man to man.
> Gone are those days . . .
> Now, in their place, behold the modern slave.

A still stronger protest against the new order he expressed in his famous—though often mocked—lines:

> Let wealth and commerce, laws and learning die,
> But leave us still our old Nobility.

Similarly Archdeacon Wilberforce (later bishop of Oxford, and remembered for his clash with T. H. Huxley over Darwinism) addressed his clergy in 1840—and was quoted in an Owenite tract. "Is it not true that there is a great and widening separation in this land between the various classes of society? . . . Where, for instance, among our vast manufacturing population, are the old bonds of mutual affection and respect—of national care on the one side and generous trust upon the other, by which the peasantry and gentry were united?" He went on to condemn the worship of property. "And has not God so ordered things, that rich and mighty nations, when they do become entangled in this idol-worship, shall become also his avengers on themselves; that the careless selfish rich shall become a prey of the untrained violent needy; that the feebleness of all human institutions, when they rest not upon God's word, shall, sooner or more late, be thoroughly proclaimed by all the horrors and agonies which wait on civil strife?"

The year 1848—the year of revolutions in Europe—was marked in England by the collapse of Chartism, by the first activity of the Christian Socialists, and the publication of John Stuart Mill's *Principles of Political Economy*. Mill, who had been brought up among the strict exponents of the individualistic economics—his father James Mill, Bentham, and Ricardo—began to find as the time went on, that his views were changing. Subsequent editions of his *Principles* became more socialistic in tone, and his *Autobiography*, published posthumously, told the story of his move towards something like the position of a convinced socialist. Ruskin, it is true, attacked Mill as a representative of the capitalist Political Economy, but this was because he used the first edition of the *Principles*. Mill saw that Chartism, although temporarily it had failed, had demonstrated that the working classes, as they grew in power and organisation, would not for ever accept a position of subordination. They would seek an increasing share in the benefits of production. Mill pointed out the advantages of co-operation, and looked to the association of labourers themselves, collectively owning the capital with which they carried on their operations. He discussed the possibilities of profit-sharing and co-partnership. These views were, in many ways, similar to those of Robert Owen, of Louis Blanc in France, and of the Christian Socialists. And Mill recognised clearly (in the second edition of the *Principles*, in 1849) that "Socialism has now become irrevocably one of the leading elements in European politics. The questions raised by it will not be set at rest by merely refusing to listen to it."

The factory reformers—Lord Shaftesbury, the Tory Richard Oastler, Parson Bull—and the Christian Socialists were prominent critics of the new industrial order. Best known of the Christian Socialists are two Church of England clergymen, Frederick Denison Maurice, a university professor, and Charles Kingsley, also a professor, a poet, and author of many novels famous in their day, including *Hypatia, Westward Ho!, Hereward the Wake*; and *The Water Babies*. Among others were the lawyer J. M. F. Ludlow, E. Vansittart Neale, a wealthy man who made funds available for co-operative undertakings, and Thomas Hughes, barrister and author of *Tom Brown's Schooldays*. All these were men of means and education. F. D. Maurice was described by Ludlow as "towering spiritually by head and shoulders over the rest", but actually it was Ludlow who suggested to Maurice the idea of starting the movement. Ludlow, who as a boy had been educated in Paris, was much influenced by French socialistic ideas, by Fourier, Lamennais, the Catholic socialism of Buchez, and Louis Blanc's democratic socialism. In 1848 Ludlow (like Owen and Marx) was an observer of the revolution in Paris, in which a half-hearted attempt was made to establish National Workshops. Impressed by the spirit of the workers in France, Ludlow returned to England, met Maurice and Kingsley, and urged on them the need to unite the Christian Church with the working classes against the evils of industrialism. The year 1848 was the year of revolutions abroad, whereas England was remarkable for having no revolution. Chartism collapsed, capitalism was evidently firmly established, and what spoke for socialism was a small movement of intellectuals, Christian, idealist, but out of touch with the mass of the workers.

The Christian Socialists began their campaign in May, 1848, with handbills, addressed to the workers disappointed by the collapse of Chartism, and with the first number of their weekly *Politics for the People*. In it Kingsley (under the pseudonym Parson Lot) addressed the Chartists: "My quarrel with the Charter is that it does not go far enough ... you mistake legislative reform for social reform, or that men's hearts can be changed by Act of Parliament." What was needed was not simply the vote but social reform on a Christian basis. But the paper, in spite of being well written by eminent contributors, only lasted a few months. Then followed, in 1850, *Tracts on Christian Socialism*, and the weekly *Christian Socialist*. Co-operation instead of competition was a guiding principle, and the Christian Socialists had their contacts with the Owenites. Indeed a number of small co-operative workshops were set up, but only existed a short time. Nevertheless the work of the Christian Socialists did help the co-operative movement as it grew up on the model of the Rochdale Society of 1844, for as a result of Christian Socialist influence the Industrial and Provident Societies Act was passed in 1852 which gave legal protection to the societies' funds. But by 1854 the Christian Socialist movement was virtually at an end; its leaders looked instead to working class education, and founded in London the Working Men's College, with Maurice as principal.

The leading idea of the Christian Socialists was to make the Christian a socialist and to make the socialist a Christian. As far as making socialism instead of competition the dominant characteristic of economic life, Maurice was at one with the Owenites. Writing about the Owenites, Maurice said: "I think they should be made to feel that communism, in whatever sense it is a principle of the New Moral World, is a most important principle of the old world and that every monastic institution—properly so-called—was a communist institution for all intents and purposes. The idea of Christian communism has been a most vigorous and generative one in all ages, and must be destined to a full development in ours." This was the ideal—a society Christian and communist—which Maurice offered in place of the competitive system which destroyed human relations between man and man.

For the Christian Socialists, like so many others, were horrified at the miseries of the capitalist world around them. Kingsley in essays and sermons, novels and poems, exposed these miseries and attacked both capitalist and landlord. In his novel *Yeast* there are some verses on the latter :

> You have sold the labouring man, Squire,
> Body and soul to shame,
> To pay for your seat in the House, Squire,
> And to pay for the feed of your game.

Bad conditions in both town and country were shown up in his *Sermons on the Cholera* in 1849. Kingsley asked if people had really repented after the last visitation—"Did they repent of and confess those sins which had caused the cholera? Did they repent of and confess the covetousness, the tyranny, the carelessness, which in most great towns, and in too many villages also, forces the poor to lodge in undrained stifling hovels, unfit for hogs, amid vapours and smells which send forth on every breath the seeds of rickets and consumption, typhus, and scarlet fever, and worse and last of all, the cholera?... Not they ... to amend them would have touched vested interests, would have cost money, the Englishman's god."

In Kingsley's *Alton Locke* (the life story of a tailor-poet) there was an exposure of the sweated labour in the London slums, particularly in the tailoring trade. Its social degradation was also the theme of his pamphlet, *Cheap Clothes and*

Nasty. In *Alton Locke*, too, there is a vision of better things to come for the poor—"Not from without, from Charters and Republics, but from within, from the Spirit working in each", and then Mammon shall fall—"Yes—Babylon the Great—the commercial world of selfish competition, drunken with the blood of God's people . . . the plutocrats and bureaucrats, the money-changers and devourers of labour". Then "labour shall be free at last, and the poor shall eat and be satisfied". And in a preface to this novel, he puts forward the remedy suggested by the early socialists for the ills of the workers. He urged the workers to adopt the principle of association. They could escape the accidents of the competitive system by taking steps "to organise among themselves associations for buying and selling the necessaries of life"; they could make their wages more valuable by buying, at little above cost price, from co-operative stores and mills.

And, in spite of the lack of immediate response to their efforts, the Christian Socialists were optimistic about the future. In 1856 Kingsley told Thomas Hughes that sometimes he had the feeling—"that the world is going right, and will go right, not your way, or my way, but its own way. Yes, we've all tried our Holloway's Pills, Tom, to cure all the ills of all the world—and we've all found out I hope by this time that the tough old world has more in its inside than any Holloway's Pills will clear out." A few weeks later the two men set out for a fishing holiday in Snowdonia on Kingsley's invitation, couched in verse :

> Leave to mournful Ruskin
> Popish Apennines,
> Dirty Stones of Venice
> And his Gas-lamps Seven;
> We've the stones of Snowdon
> And the lamps of heaven.

John Ruskin, mournful or not—though today we know something of his mental suffering and tortured private life, made his own contribution to the criticism of the social order and to proposals for socialistic reforms. Born in the year of Peterloo, and dying in the year which marked the beginnings of the Labour Party, his life spans both the earlier socialist movement and the later revival of socialism towards the end of the century. But he stands somewhat outside the main course of the movement, and his influence was slight—as E. R. Pease and Bernard Shaw pointed out— on the Fabian Society, so influential in the development of Labour policy. He was, nevertheless, a powerful voice. A wealthy man, with an independent position as a famous writer and art critic, he could speak out freely. His *Modern Painters, The Seven Lamps of Architecture*, and *The Stones of Venice* had given him a great reputation. His books influenced William Morris, whose socialism was a religion of fellowship. Art for Art's sake was not enough for such men, and out of Ruskin's love of art itself there developed a social consciousness. He saw a connection between a people's character and its art; he believed that the great and beautiful monuments of the past were created by men who worshipped some worthy principle or ideal, and from this he went on to regard the industrial towns, the railways, stations, factories, with their ugliness and squalor, as the work of men who worshipped Mammon and were activated solely by a love of gain. Nor could the effect of all this on the life of the workers be disregarded. Art should serve humanity by the presentation of noble ideas, and there was little of nobility in the outward manifestation of industrialism. And behind his view of art was his religious belief. The idea of theocratic government of nature and of human life naturally tended towards a view of the state as paternal. Authority and obedience were important, and he looked to the authority of the state as the means to the carrying out of a policy for the social good.

About 1859 he was turning more and more to social

activity. As he declared at this time : "For my own part I feel the force of mechanism and the fury of avaricious commerce to be at present so irresistible that I have seceded from the study not only of architecture, but nearly of all art, and have given myself, as I would in a besieged city, to seek the best modes of getting bread and butter for its multitudes." And it was not only commerce itself which was so irresistible, but also the theory of commerce—the prevalent popular beliefs which backed up and rationalised the advances of capitalism. A reviewer of Ruskin's *Unto this Last* put it plainly that "the masters have the upper hand of the men" and then supplied the justification : "political economy adds the information that to deprive them of this advantage by Legislation would diminish the power of producing wealth".

Nowhere does Ruskin give a full, clear, and entirely consistent statement of his social principles. They are scattered throughout his various works; he was very ready, too, to allow full rein to his fancy in following up any clue in literature or mythology which seemed suggestive of his conclusions. But there does seem to have been a more comprehensive threefold scheme at the back of his mind. In *Unto this Last* he attacked the basis of the accepted Political Economy; in *Munera Pulveris* he sought to replace it with a new scheme of Social Economy; while in *Time and Tide* he attempted to show what he conceived the true social order might be.

In his attack on the current political economy he does not mince his words, and, like Lord John Manners, looked back to a supposed better world in the past. He writes in one of his letters : "The Science of Political Economy is a lie— wholly and to the very root (as hitherto taught). It is also the damnedest—that is to say, the most utterly and to the lowest pit condemned of God and his angels—that the Devil, or Betrayer of Men, has yet invented, except his (the Devil's) theory of Sanctification. To this 'Science', and to this alone (the professed and organised pursuit of money) is owing all the evil of modern days. I say all. The Monastic theory is at an end. It is now the Money theory which corrupts the Church, corrupts the household life, destroys honour, beauty, and life throughout the universe. It is the death incarnate of Modernism, and the so-called science of its pursuit is the most cretinous, speechless, paralysing plague that has yet touched the brains of mankind."

Ruskin's attack in *Unto this Last* upon the current Political Economy is directed towards showing that it has wrongfully assumed that title and thus is in reality nothing more than a science of Commercial Wealth. He draws a distinction between what he considers actually is, and what should be recognised as, the science of political economy. He does not deny that there is a science according to the older economists but its principles are not those conducive to the good of the state as a whole, it could scarcely then be said to be a science of *political* economy. "Political economy," he says, "(the economy of a State or of citizens) consists simply in the production, preservation, and distribution, at fittest time and place, of useful or pleasurable things. The farmer who cuts his hay at the right time; the shipwright who drives his bolts well home in sound wood; the builder who lays good bricks in well-tempered mortar; the housewife who takes care of her furniture in the parlour, and guards against all waste in her kitchen; and the singer who rightly disciplines, and never overstrains her voice, are all political economists in the true and final sense : adding continually to the riches and well-being of the nation to which they belong." Ruskin's fundamental principle is that Political Economy, in his sense, must have as its object the maintenance and good of the whole state.

Ruskin realised the difference between wealth and welfare. The advance to such a state where welfare would be the fundamental of society is to be by individual rather than by public action, but Ruskin did put forward some practical proposals, as "the worst of the political creed at which I wish to arrive". The reforms which he advocated were :

1. National Schools for the young. Government cost and Government discipline.
2. Every child to be taught a trade or calling.
3. In connection with these, Government workshops where "good and exemplary work should be done, and pure and true substance sold".
4. Any unemployed to be set to work in these workshops.
5. Such work to be payed for at a fixed rate in each employment.
6. Penal work for those who would not otherwise work.
7. For the old and destitute, comfort to be provided.

The tentative way in which Ruskin puts forward these suggestions and his appeal to individual rather than to public action show that he was not entirely separated from an enlightened individualism.

In *Munera Pulveris* and *Time and Tide* Ruskin developed his socialistic thinking further. In the latter work he suggests that the labourers should organise themselves into guilds. This would amount to the transformation of trade unions into guilds for the carrying on of production. Ruskin does not go very deeply into the constitution of these guilds and does not explain how they are to be instituted. But it is implied both in *Time and Tide* and *Fors Clavigera* that voluntary co-operation of individuals is to be the basis. Then the guilds might gradually supersede the capitalist employer. The guild, however, was not immediately or by law to replace the individual "captain of industry". Outside the guilds competition was to be allowed so as to preserve that "erratic external ingenuity as cannot be tested by law". The producing guilds were to control the retailers. Also "necessary public works and undertakings, as roads, mines, harbour protections, and the like" were to be owned and administered for the public profit.

Membership of the guilds was to be optional, and one particularly Ruskinian feature directed towards the securing of a high standard of craftsmanship was to be the joint responsibility of the guild for the qualities of the wares made by its members. In this respect Ruskin is harking back to the medieval craft-guild.

Ruskin's treatment of agriculture was marked by a combination of tempered feudalism and state-control. He did not advocate nationalisation of the land, but there was to be fixity of rent and security for the tenants' improvements. The land was worked into his idea of governing classes, and from it came not only landed proprietors, but soldiers, lawyers, and state functionaries. He also adds a class of "bishops" or overseers, whose duty it was to supervise and see that no member should "suffer from unknown want or live in unrecognised crime". His state functionaries were to be drawn from the landed classes—Ruskin is a believer in aristocracy—but beyond this he is not greatly concerned with the political form of government.

In addition to his theory Ruskin was also responsible for several practical attempts at the working of his ideas, as far as was possible to one individual. He initiated reforms in landlordism in conjunction with Miss Octavia Hill (daughter of James Hill, a supporter of Robert Owen), by improvements in the working-class dwellings on his property in London. As a publisher and book-seller he carried on business in accordance with his principles, and with proper regard for the conditions of his work people. His largest experiment was that of the Guild of St George, a company he started with the idea of forming an ideal agricultural community. It failed largely because Ruskin was unable to gain sufficient support, nor were the group of people he settled on the land easy to find or successful in practice. As Mr Hobson has pointed out—"No notion is more fatuous than the quite common one that since labour and land are the prime requisites for the maintenance of life, any labour put on any land can earn for the labourers a sufficient livelihood".

All the efforts—Owen's communities, O'Connor's Chartist Land Plan, and other 'back to the land' schemes, the work of the Christian Socialists and of Ruskin—and all the thinking of the early socialists produced, at this time, little or no immediate effect. Efforts and theorising did not crystallise into a socialist movement. Capitalism was firmly established, and remained unshaken. After the failure of Chartism, working class leaders inclined to work with the Liberals. Indeed there had been already many improvements and reforms: the first effective Factory Act (1833), the Mines Act prohibiting the employment of women and girls underground, the Ten Hours day, reduction of the stamp tax on newspapers, the repeal of the Corn Laws (1846). Beginnings had been made with trade unionism and co-operation, and the workers had learnt that the authorities and the existing order were strong, that any grand attempt to replace the existing order at one go was doomed to failure. When the franchise was extended in 1867, the workers backed Gladstone; they were not drawn away—at least not until 1874—by Disraeli's social Toryism or the revolutionary method of Karl Marx. Some of the former Chartists seem to have been satisfied with the Liberal measures and with the growth of democracy, the fulfilment of their earlier dreams. Did they, by abandoning separate working class action at the political level and working with the Liberals, take the wrong turning? When, much later, the history of Chartism came to be written it was often written from the socialist point of view. To such writers it seemed that the development of the Labour Party was inevitable, in the natural course of social development. But was this so? In the last decades of the nineteenth century, working class MPs sat with the Liberals, and were known as "Lib-Lab." It might seem, too, that in any capitalist country a Labour Party must arise. Yet in capitalist

America such a party did not arise. It could be argued, indeed, that when, later on, the working classes abandoned the Liberal Party, it was then that they took the wrong turning—that but for that there might have been a single, strong, and united progressive party in this country.

4. Marx and Marxism

MEANWHILE KARL MARX appears—though his influence was much greater on the Continent than in Britain. Eventually he emerged as the greatest figure in the history of socialism from among a large number of other socialistic writers and thinkers—many of them remarkable men in their day, and some not yet forgotten—Saint-Simon and his followers, Fourier, Sismondi, Ledru Rollin, Louis Blanc, Blanqui, Bakunin, Weitling, Proudhon, Lassalle. With other socialists Marx was often involved in bitter controversy, and would overwhelm his adversaries by his vast erudition, his subtle and ruthless thinking, and the strength of his personality and intellectual powers. Though there might be something about him of the German schoolmaster, dogmatic and completely confident in his own knowledge and ability to set it out, he had also the Prussian virtues of a sense of duty, hard work, sobriety, devotion to the task in hand, and utter perseverance in carrying it out. For the mass of the writings of Marx and Engels—some thirty-nine solid volumes in the German edition produced by the Institute for Marxism-Leninism—some of them with curious and puzzling titles such as *The Holy Family, The German Ideology,* or the *Theses on Feuerbach*, there emerged as particularly important in the history of socialism, *The Communist Manifesto* and *Das Kapital.* And Marx himself eventually appeared as more than the leading figure in the history of socialism, as more than a philosopher and economist. At his funeral in Highgate cemetery his lifelong friend, Engels, declared : "His mission in life was to contribute in one way or another to the over-throw of capitalist society." With the Russian Revolution thirty-four years later Marx took his place, not merely as a leading figure in the history of socialism, but as a figure of importance in history itself. One might well ask indeed: Did Karl Marx make the Russian Revolution, or did the Russian Revolution make Karl Marx?

Born in Germany in 1818 and dying in London in 1883 Marx's personal life was less important than his ideas; his life was devoted to study and writing. His father practised as a lawyer in Trier, in the German Rhineland which after 1815 became a part of Prussia : he was a Jew, but joined the Lutheran church before Karl's birth. Karl went to school in Trier, and then studied at the universities of Bonn and Berlin. He attended lectures on law but became more and more absorbed by philosophy and history. He worked for a radical journal in Cologne, and became its editor. The paper was suppressed by the government in 1843, but Marx was able to move to a similar position in Paris, and there during 1843-5 his socialist interests developed. But in 1845 Marx was expelled from Paris, and moved to Brussels. Then came the excitements and the traumatic experience of 1848, the year of revolutions. All over Europe there were revolts, nationalist or liberal, against foreign oppressors or monarchical regimes : in Paris, in Naples, Milan, Rome, Venice, in Berlin, Vienna, Budapest. Marx was back in Paris, then off to Cologne where he started a journal once more until expelled in 1849, then back to Paris. But by this time the revolution in Paris was almost over—it had come near to a social revolution when the workers raised their barricades in June 1848 and fought in the streets against the troops of the Republican government. But the workers had failed and Marx could not stay in Paris. In August he took refuge in

London, where he lived, until his death, absorbed in his studies in the British Museum, and in his socialist activity. His family life was happy, in spite of his poverty. With Friedrich Engels (1820-1895), son of a wealthy German manufacturer, Marx enjoyed a close friendship of nearly forty years. Engels worked in England and made a close study of English conditions. He supplied Marx with much information and assistance, and also with financial help; after the death of Marx, Engels compiled the second and third volumes of *Kapital*.

After he was expelled from Paris in 1845, Marx was in constant contact with socialist and revolutionary groups, especially exiled German artisans, both in Brussels and in London. Such groups were loosely linked in the Communist League which had succeeded the earlier League of the Just. There was a general expectation of a coming revolution. At a meeting in London of the Communist League late in 1847 Marx and Engels were commissioned to prepare a party programme. This they did, and early in 1848, a few weeks before the revolution broke out in Paris, a London printer produced the original German version of *The Communist Manifesto*. It was, therefore, from the start an international production; years later it was described as "undoubtedly the most wide-spread, the most international production of all socialist literature, the common platform acknowledged by millions of working men from Siberia to California". Later, too, Engels explained why the programme was called communist and not socialist. It was because the term socialist was regarded as Utopian, and Engels maintained that "whatever portion of the working class had become convinced of the insufficiency of mere political revolutions, and had proclaimed the necessity of a total social change, called itself Communist".

Thus the importance of the *Manifesto* was clear in the eyes of its producers. And it still remains the most clear and concise of communist statements. "It was only with Marx

and Engels" said Bertrand Russell, "that socialism reached
intellectual maturity." And of *The Communist Manifesto*
he said that it contained all the essentials of their doctrine.
"The greatest of all socialist pamphlets," Sir Isaiah Berlin
has called it, "a document of prodigious dramatic force."

"A spectre is haunting Europe—the spectre of Communism," so the *Manifesto* began. "All the powers of old
Europe have entered into a holy alliance to exorcise this
spectre : Pope and Tsar, Metternich and Guizot, French
Radicals and German police spies." And so "it is high time
that Communists should openly, in the face of the whole
world, publish their views, their aims, their tendencies, and
meet this nursery tale of the spectre of Communism with a
manifesto of the party itself".

First the *Manifesto* stated the existence of the class war—
"The history of all hitherto existing society is the history of
class struggles . . . freeman and slave, patrician and plebeian,
lord and serf . . . oppressor and oppressed" and the development of modern industry had simplified the older struggles.
"Our epoch, the epoch of the bourgeoisie, possesses, however,
this distinctive feature : it has simplified the class antagon-
isms. Society as a whole is more and more splitting up into
two great hostile camps, into two great classes directly facing
each other—bourgeoisie and proletariat." By bourgeoisie was
meant the capitalists, who owned the means of production;
by proletariat the wage-labourers who, owning no productive resources, sell their labour power. It was explained how
the bourgeoisie had developed out of feudalism; how, in its
time, it had been a revolutionary force destroying the feudal
order out of which it had grown. "The bourgeoisie . . . has
put an end to all feudal, patriarchal, idyllic relations. . . . It
has resolved personal worth into exchange value . . . In one
word, for exploitation, veiled by religious and political
illusions, it has substituted naked, shameless, direct, brutal
exploitation."

"The bourgeoisie, during its rule of scarce one hundred

years, has created more massive and more colossal productive forces than have all preceding generations together ... machinery, application of chemistry to industry and agriculture, steam navigation, railways, electric telegraphs, clearing of whole continents for cultivation"; it has spread over the world in its search for constantly expanding markets, and has forced capitalist production on hitherto barbarous lands; it has created enormous urban areas, and subjected the countryside to the rule of the towns; it has centralised the means of production, concentrated property into a few hands, and also centralised political control by bringing loosely connected provinces together under one government.

But bourgeois society has its fatal weaknesses. "Modern bourgeois society ... is like the sorcerer who is no longer able to control the powers of the nether world whom he has called up by his spells." Recurrent commercial crises put the very existence of bourgeois society in danger, and in such crises "there breaks out an epidemic that, in all earlier epochs, would have seemed an absurdity—the epidemic of over-production". And as the bourgeoisie has developed, so also has developed the proletariat. As industry developed, so the proletariat increased in number—"it becomes concentrated in greater masses, its strength grows, and it feels that strength more". The workers struggle to protect themselves, they form trade unions, and sometimes they break out into revolt. Improved means of communication bring workers in one part of the country into touch with those in another; this leads to ever expanding union of the workers. The workers, too, may be helped by divisions in the bourgeoisie itself, and the bourgeoisie in its struggles with the older aristocratic order or with foreign countries may have to appeal for the assistance of the proletariat. Throughout there is a "more or less veiled civil war raging within existing society". And the authors of the *Manifesto* see an increasing misery for the workers. Whereas the slave and the serf had a modicum of security, "the modern labourer, on the contrary, instead of rising with the progress of industry, sinks deeper and deeper below the conditions of existence of his own class. He becomes a pauper, and pauperism develops more rapidly than population and wealth". And so it becomes evident that the bourgeoisie is no longer fit to be the ruling class in society. Now comes the time for the proletariat to step in.

"The essential condition for the existence and for the sway of the bourgeois class is the formation and augmentation of capital; the condition for capital is wage-labour. Wage-labour rests exclusively on competition between the labourers. The advance of industry, whose involuntary promoter is the bourgeoisie, replaces the isolation of the labourers, due to competition, by their revolutionary combination, due to association. The development of modern industry, therefore, cuts from under its feet the very foundation on which the bourgeoisie produces and appropriates products. What the bourgeoisie therefore produces, above all, are its own grave-diggers. Its fall and the victory of the proletariat are equally inevitable." Thus the proletarian revolution was forecast as the culminating and inevitable result of a long historical development.

In the second section of the *Manifesto* the authors defined the nature of the Communists as a group and their relation to a proletariat as a whole. "The Communists do not form a separate party opposed to other working class parties . . . but they always and everywhere represent the interests of the movement as a whole." They are the spearhead of the working class movement, "the most advanced and resolute section of the working class parties of every country . . . clearly understanding the line of march, the conditions, and the ultimate general results of the proletarian movement". Their aims are: "formation of the proletariat into a class, overthrow of the bourgeois supremacy, conquest of political power by the proletariat".

Possible objections are answered—in a way calculated to delight the working class and cover the bourgeoisie with

ridicule. Will private property be abolished? Only bourgeois property (that is property accumulated through capitalist exploitation of labour) will be abolished—and already,
under the bourgeois regime, the immense majority of people
have no property. Will individuality disappear? If by individual is meant the bourgeois, the middle class owner of
property, "this person must indeed be swept out of the way".
And culture? This is nothing but a bourgeois concept, based
on its own bourgeois notions of freedom, culture, law.
Abolition of the family? The Communists are accused of
this. But on what is the bourgeois family based? "The
bourgeois sees in his wife a mere instrument of production."
He makes free with the wives and daughters of the proletariat, with prostitutes, and he and his fellows "take the
greatest pleasure in seducing each other's wives". And one's
country—have the Communists no patriotism? "The working men have no country. We cannot take from them what
they have not got." What about eternal truths—freedom,
justice, morality, religion? "The Communist revolution is
the most radical rupture with traditional property relations;
no wonder that its development involves the most radical
rupture with traditional ideas."

The *Manifesto* then put forward a number of proposals
for immediate action by the proletariat when in power. They
included :

Abolition of property in land.
Heavy, graduated income tax.
Abolition of inheritance.
Centralisation of credit in a state bank.
Transport and communication to be centralised by the
    state.
Extension of state ownership of factories.
Obligation on all to work.
Free education for all children.

Then, when "class distinctions have disappeared, and all production has been concentrated in the hands ... of the nation, the public power will lose its political character"— (that is, the state will fade away)—"we shall have an association in which the free development of each is the condition for the free development of all".

Later on, in section three, the authors criticised the writings of earlier socialist groups and dismissed the work of St Simon, Fourier, and Robert Owen as Utopian; in section four they stated the Communist position in relation to the opposition parties of their time. And in particular: "the Communists turn their attention chiefly to Germany, because that country is on the eve of a bourgeois revolution that is bound to be carried out under more advanced conditions of European civilisation and with a much more developed proletariat than that of England was in the seventeenth, and of France in the eighteenth century, and because the bourgeois revolution in Germany will be but the prelude to an immediately following proletarian revolution".

Then the *Manifesto* closed: "The Communists disdain to conceal their views and aims. They openly declare that their ends can be attained only by the forcible overthrow of all existing social conditions. Let the ruling classes tremble at a Communist revolution. The proletarians have nothing to lose but their chains. They have a world to win.

"Working men of all countries, unite!"

Thus Marx and Engels produced what they regarded as a scientific theory of socialism, and it was their theory that established the revolutionary seizure of power as the necessary means to the realisation of socialism. Their theory, as stated concisely and with arresting originality in the *Manifesto*, depended on the materialist conception of history, or, as it is sometimes called, dialectical materialism or economic determinism, and was supported in later years by Marx's major work, *Capital*. Marx's dialectical materialism is implicit in Marx's writing—it is not formally expounded in any one work. Marx was much influenced by Hegel and his view of historical development—that the process of reasoning in the mind is the primary reality and the historical process reflects it. Marx put this the other way round—that the movement in things (i.e. history) comes first, and the movement of thought is its reflection. Marx claimed that he put Hegel's dialectic right side up. "What else does the history of ideas prove" the *Manifesto* asked, "than that intellectual production changes its character in proportion as material production is changed? The ruling ideas of each age have ever been the ideas of its ruling class." Basic to all was man's need to get a living—and his means of doing it, his powers of production, determined the kind of society in which he lived. There was, too, in history something of the stages in a logical or dialectic controversy: thesis, anti-thesis, and synthesis; Marx saw class struggles in this way—bourgeoisie, proletariat, the new socialist order. The materialist conception of history, in popular form, proved most attractive to the working class, as did also the labour theory of value and the theory of surplus value which Marx developed in *Capital*. This work is, in effect, a detailed study of economics, of the process of capitalist production, with a large amount of economic history which allows the reader to follow the historical development of modern industry. The labour theory of value—that the value of a commodity depends on the amount of labour put into its production—was not invented by Marx. It was to be found in Adam Smith and Ricardo (and it was held by Robert Owen and other socialist writers before the Marxists). But as worked out by Marx, it became an important part of socialist theory. The theory of surplus value maintains that the worker produces more than is necessary for his subsistence, but he is paid only a subsistence wage; the surplus or difference between what he produces and what he gets is taken by the capitalist—again a theory welcome to critics of the capitalist system (it had been suggested already by Hodgskin and Thompson) and making an immediate appeal to the poor and over-worked.

Capital, however, for years after the publication of the first volume in 1867, was available only to those who could read German or French. Hyndman and Belfort Bax were influenced by it. But the *Communist Manifesto* had appeared in an English translation in 1850 in the periodical *Red Republican*, edited by the Chartist, George Julian Harvey. Yet the teachings of Marx never had in England the influence they had elsewhere. British traditions had a strength of their own, and there was a dislike of foreign ideas; religion, especially Nonconformity, had its special hold on the people; and democratic government and the social services increasingly redressed the social balance. Marx was—as, indeed, are we all—a man of his time. He was by no means unique in feeling the influence on human affairs of the powers of production. The writer of an economic tract, from the orthodox point of view, had clearly pointed out as early as 1830 the advantages of machinery; he asked his readers "to reflect on the means which have raised mankind to their actual state of knowledge, of civilisation, and of comparative comforts; and he is confident of their being convinced that the whole progress is entirely owing to the invention of contrivances for facilitating labour and rendering it more productive". And almost at the same time a writer in the *Quarterly Review* was noting that the changes going on, far from creating class differences, were tending "to approximate the lower classes to the higher ... it is obvious in dress, manners, and acquirements". As time went on this approximation became greater. Many things, too, cut across class distinctions—national feeling (it just was not true that "the working men have no country"—Marx as a German had no sympathy with the Slavs of the Austrian Empire), churches and chapels, games, amusements. The development of industry produced, besides a capitalist class and a proletariat, a buffer between them with the growth of a clerical and administrative class. Increasing misery turned out to be a myth—the lot of the workers improved greatly. Nor did capitalists become so few that they could be easily expropriated; they became more numerous. As shareholders in joint-stock companies innumerable individuals became interested in the capitalist system. The socialist revolution was not inevitable, as Marx supposed; the proletarian revolution in Germany which he forecast did not take place (unless indeed Marx looked forward prophetically to the Nazi revolution of 1933!). Revolution, too, can produce its own horrors and defeat its object. The German so-called True Socialists, whom Marx dismissed, had pointed out that a bloody class war and revolution would lead to a tyranny exercised by the victorious proletariat. Indeed, as Bertrand Russell has pointed out, history shows many examples of decay as well as of progress—capitalism and war may bring barbarism not communism: "the dogmatic optimism of the Communist doctrine must be regarded as a relic of Victorianism". With regard to England, however, Marx appeared to make an exception. According to Engels (writing a preface in 1886 to the first English translation of *Capital*), Marx concluded that "at least in Europe, England is the only country where the inevitable social revolution might be effected entirely by peaceful and legal means"— though Marx had added that he hardly expected the English ruling classes to submit without a pro-slavery rebellion.

PART II

5. The Revival of Socialism

THERE IS SOMETHING of a gap in the history of British Socialism between the activities of Robert Owen (and a little later of the Christian Socialists) and the revival of socialism in the 1880s. "Only the closest inspection of the British political scene," Mr Henry Pelling points out, "affords any indication of socialist activity in 1880" and the little interest there was came from abroad, from the success of the German Social Democratic Party—much under the influence of Marx—in winning thirteen seats in the Reichstag in 1877. It is true that the writings of Ruskin bridge the gap (and there were British trade union representatives in the First International), but there was no socialist movement in this country. To some extent the reasons for working class militancy were less urgent. Capitalism was firmly established, and in spite of the early miseries and the enduring hardships for many, the wealth and prosperity of the country were increasing greatly. "If," as Professor Ashworth has said of the mid-Victorian period, "the accumulation of wealth and its application to further accumulation is taken as the criterion of economic success, then this was a very successful age." Many of the working class saw their own interest in this rising prosperity—in the trade unions, in co-operative societies, and in friendly societies and mutual aid societies of various kinds. And the working classes—at least so far as the extension of the franchise went—had found a champion in the Liberal leader, Gladstone, though it was Disraeli who had carried the Act of 1867. The Reforms Acts of 1867 and 1884 had given the vote to the people—though it was a long time before the masses realised their power. The personality of great men also played a part in postponing the growth of socialism or of independent working class activity. Gladstone and Disraeli (later Lord Beaconsfield) captured the imagination of the country; each, in his different way, was a man of genius. They generated the strongest feelings, families were split, and friend divided from friend—and it was the personality of the leaders which was the motivating force; as one writer put it (in 1878) "it is all purely personal, the divergence of opinion not being so much upon the merits of the questions which seem seldom understood, but upon the feelings that are entertained either towards Lord Beaconfield or Mr Gladstone". Such feelings endured for many years—an intense reverence for Gladstone, admiration for Disraeli, matched by their detractors who dismissed Gladstone as a hypocrite pretending to act according to God's will and Disraeli as a devious oriental without principle or serious purpose. But by 1884 Gladstone's work for the people was largely done—even at the end of Gladstone's first government in 1874 Disraeli had mocked the Liberal ministers as "exhausted volcanoes". And in the 1870s a change in Britain's economic position of strength began to appear: agriculture suffered depression as a result of greatly increased imports of foreign food, and Britain's overseas competitors were beginning to catch up.

Britain, however, had passed through the fundamental economic and social changes of industrialisation and at the same time established a democratic system of government, without violent revolution. This was a very considerable achievement. Nevertheless there were causes enough for discontent, in the long hours and hard lives of the working people, and in the grinding poverty of the badly paid or those with only casual employment. Towards the end of the century a careful inquiry made by a retired shipowner, Charles Booth, the first volume of whose *Life and Labour of the People of London* was published in 1889, showed that in London 30 per cent of the population of the world's richest city lived in poverty. Their food, clothes, and housing were not enough to keep them in a decent physical condition. And similar inquiries were made in other cities. It became clear that all industrial towns contained many people, chiefly in the unskilled labourer class, who lived in want, ill-health, and misery. Farm labourers, too, were in a bad way; their pay was about half that of factory hands, and as they could not easily combine in a union to protect themselves, they were more liable to tyrannical treatment by their masters.

The workers had formed trade unions with the immediate intention of advancing their interests, by improving wages, hours, and conditions of labour. While the individual labourer was powerless to improve his conditions, when a number of labourers combined into a union they could bargain with an employer. When the unions grew in size and strength, they were able—once the town artisans had got the vote by the Reform Act of 1867—to exert pressure on the government. They were able to do this in spite of a good deal of criticism, opposition, and resistance from the employers and the well-to-do generally, and not surprisingly unions did not always act in the best or wisest way. There were, indeed, some deeds of violence by unionists against non-unionists, to make them join and pay the subscription. Eventually in the 1870s both Gladstone and Disraeli found themselves forced to give attention to the making of laws to regulate and improve the trade union position. Unions were given protection against embezzlement of their funds, just as the property of any other lawful association of people was protected; they were freed from the old common law against conspiracy which had made their legal position difficult and uncertain if they organised a strike, and they were allowed peaceful picketing during strikes.

The unions began to meet together in an annual Trades Union Congress in 1868. The election of 1874 brought to the House of Commons the first working-class MPs, Thomas Burt and Alexander Macdonald, who were miners. Both were elected as Liberals. The son of a Lanarkshire miner, Macdonald had started to work in the pit when eight years old. As a young man he had saved enough to go to Glasgow University, and became a teacher for a few years. But he devoted most of his life to helping the miners—he was elected president of the National Union of Miners in 1863. The Miners' Conference of that year opened with prayer—an interesting feature which illustrates the religious outlook typical of their leaders, mostly Nonconformists—and under Macdonald's lead they worked out their programme of reform. The miners aimed at a reduction of hours, better conditions of work, an end to the truck system (payment of wages partly in kind), and the right of the men to appoint checkweighers, that is their own representatives who checked the amount of coal produced, on which each man's pay was based. Later, in 1889, the London dockers organised a strike for higher pay, and won. This, and other strikes of poorly paid workers, created considerable public sympathy.

The co-operative movement—of stores or shops run by working class people for the working classes—was also growing into an important organisation. The idea went back to the Owenites. But the modern movement is usually traced to the shop in Toad Lane, Rochdale, in 1844. The shops or stores spread through Lancashire and Yorkshire, into Scotland and the Midlands, and lastly to the more conservative London and the southern counties. In 1863 the Co-operative Wholesale Society started in Manchester. This organisation was formed by the retail co-operative shops to make wholesale purchases on their behalf; the wholesale organisation, since it made bulk purchases, could usually buy more cheaply than a single small shop could. The CWS went along rather slowly for twenty years, but eventually became a very large trading organisation.

The co-operative movement helped the working classes in at least three ways : the retail stores gave good value for money; the profit was shared among members according to the value of their purchases, and this share or dividend could be left to accumulate at interest, so encouraging thrift; and the stores encouraged democracy, for each store was managed by a committee elected by the members of the local co-operative society. In addition, the co-operative movement turned some of its profits to educational ends, such as classes for its members. Business profit and educational advance were allied; hard-headed common sense was not divorced from social idealism.

Once more the idea of socialism began to make an appeal. The term "Christian Socialist" was heard again in the 1880s, and there were inside the Church of England organisations such as the Guild of St Matthew and the Christian Social Union striving for greater social responsibility and challenging economic evils. Of course, in good times people did not listen much to socialist arguments. When industry was expanding and there were plenty of jobs, there was little socialism. But when things went badly, people began to think about socialism. In 1875 the agricultural depression set in. The home market was flooded, and cheap grain began to pour in from the vast, newly developed wheatfields of the United States, fields large enough to make full use of the combine harvester, at that time little used in Britain. The new railways in America and Atlantic shipping—both sail and steam—brought the grain to Britain in great quantities, where it could be sold more cheaply than British grain. British prices dropped. Refrigeration also enabled overseas producers to send meat and butter to be sold in Britain, although British livestock farming suffered very little. The depression became even worse in 1891-2. There was unemployment and distress.

Younger men could leave the countryside and look for work in the towns, or emigrate. But it was not so easy to find work in the towns; for in the 1880s there was periodic depression in industry as well as in agriculture. Britain had had a good period as workshop of the world; the Industrial Revolution had taken place there first and given her a good start. Germany and America, however, were now fast developing their own industries, and beginning to compete with British manufactured goods. People were being made to realise that industrial expansion and consequent prosperity were not necessarily to go on for ever. And, more than anything else, unemployment was likely to make the workers listen to socialist arguments and hope to find in them a remedy for their distress.

Disraeli, as a young man, had contrasted the two nations —the two social classes of rich and poor—which existed in England. He had implied his own "conviction that the rights of labour were as sacred as those of property ... that the social happiness of the millions should be the first object of a statesman". Soon after Disraeli, Karl Marx was writing in the *Communist Manifesto*: "More and more, society is splitting into two great hostile camps, into two great and directly contraposed classes: bourgeoisie and proletariat." Marx—to summarise his doctrine—developed his idea of the class war: the rich against the poor. He argued that the rich get richer by exploiting the poor, and the poor get poorer. The wealth of the rich would come to be concentrated into fewer and fewer hands; great monopolies would grow up, and small businesses disappear. The workers would be more and more exploited, and their lot would be one of increasing misery. But inevitably with the growth of large-scale production, the factory system would bring them together in large numbers; the workers would unite. At last they would break out in a violent revolution; they would overthrow the capitalists, seize control of the monopolies, and work the industrial system themselves and for themselves. It was on the Continent that Marx's theory had immense influence; it was taken up by Lenin and lay behind the Russian Revolution of 1917. It was Marx who—though not of the working class—set the working class on the path of violent revolution.

Marx's theories, however, had little effect in Britain. They did not interfere with the slow, measured development of British institutions: the steady growth of a democratic system in central and local government, and the gradual improvement of social conditions both by law and as a result of public opinion. Many workers' leaders considered that, as private enterprise was creating great wealth, it was better to work with it rather than against it. Nor did the rich, the capitalists, become fewer. As joint-stock companies with limited liability grew up, a large number of small shareholders invested in industry and became capitalists. And so there were more capitalists as capitalism developed in Britain, not fewer as Marx had supposed.

There was, however, in Britain one Marxist group which thought in terms of class conflict and a working-class revolution to overthrow the governing class. This group was the Social Democratic Federation, which began in 1881 as the Democratic Federation. Its founder was H. M. Hyndman (1841-1921) who on a trip to America had studied Marx's *Capital* in a French translation. William Morris, the artist, craftsman and poet, was a member for a short time, as was Marx's daughter, Eleanor, until at the end of 1884 they left to found the Socialist League. The SDF organised some large meetings and marches of the unemployed during the winter of 1885-86, and put up some candidates for parliament. But the socialists' disagreements and lack of public support made the movement ineffective.

Hyndman, the moving force, was a most unusual socialist. He was possessed of considerable wealth, his father was at Eton and Trinity, Cambridge, and he himself was a Trinity man. He was acquainted with everyone, had been a friend

of Mazzini and Garibaldi, and knew Kropotkin and Karl
Marx; he recognised in Disraeli's *Sybil* "the same current of
ideas that affected Carlyle, Ruskin, Kingsley", and he noted
Disraeli's early sympathy with the Chartists—he had a long
interview with Disraeli, a few weeks before the old statesman
died, and discussed with him the socialist policy which
Hyndman was turning over in his mind. He had visited
many parts of the world as a traveller and journalist, and
had seen something of its horrors and oppressions. He sided
with the under-dog, and this brought him to socialism. He
found, as he wrote later, in the years before he started his
organisation, that "there was no effective socialism whatever
in Great Britain . . . public opinion was bitterly hostile . . .
and every socialist was regarded as a bomb-thrower and an
incendiary". The ascendancy of Gladstone—what Hyndman
called "the unreasoning hero-worship which the Liberals felt
for Mr Gladstone" making him "a sanctified leader immune
from criticism"—was the dominant political factor. But
Hyndman's efforts did something to revive an interest in
socialism and to encourage discussion of socialist ideas. A
pamphlet *Socialism Made Plain* was published, and a weekly
Justice. William Morris in his *Dream of John Ball* (1888)
and *News from Nowhere* (1890) produced something of
more than ephemeral interest. In a letter of 1883 Morris,
who was influenced by Ruskin, Carlyle, and J. S. Mill, and
had also tackled *Capital, wrote* : "The contrasts of rich and
poor are unendurable and ought not to be endured by either
rich or poor. Now it seems to me that, feeling this, I am
bound to act for the destruction of the system which seems
to me mere oppression and obstruction; such a system can
only be destroyed, it seems to me, by the united discontent
of numbers . . . in other words the antagonism of classes,
which the system has bred, is the natural and necessary
instrument of its destruction" and the present system "will
give place to socialism". Hyndman had observed in the
United States in the 1870s and 1880s devastating economic

crises and the wholesale unemployment which they brought. He was led to think in terms of class war and coming revolution. But, writing many years later, he admitted that "the class war has not reached the stage of revolutionary class crisis so quickly as I then anticipated. The wheels of economics do grind slowly though they grind exceeding small."

The Fabian Society, founded in 1884, which was less impressed by Marxian ideas, was more influential in this country. Among its members were the dramatist, Bernard Shaw, and the social historians, Sidney and Beatrice Webb. The Fabians took their name from the Roman general, Fabius, who had believed in fighting Hannibal by a cautious policy of gradual advances rather than by a pitched battle : they believed that socialism could come about gradually by peaceful and democratic means. To this end they set about infiltrating their ideas into the existing parties, Conservative and Liberal, and also educating public opinion by means of publications such as the *Fabian Essays*, by meetings and discussion, and by working in local government and getting their ideas slowly adopted. Bernard Shaw dealt in his plays with many topical social issues; by making people laugh at abuses and follies he awakened their power of criticism and stimulated ideas of social reform.

Many other influences also helped to awaken people to a realisation of social evils and made them think of socialism as a solution. One of these influences was the writer, Robert Blatchford. He was an ex-soldier, who had a gift for vigorous and effective writing. He started a very popular socialist weekly, the *Clarion*, in 1891. Even today one can read his books—*Merrie England* and *Britain for the British*—with enjoyment and interest. He did not hate the rich so much as feel genuine sympathy for the poor and the under-dog. He was an attractive character, and he aroused considerable popular attention for he made socialism seem both plausible and attractive, something which could be economically effective and something which was not merely a foreign theory, but English through and through. As he wrote in *Merrie England* : "Socialists point out that if all the industries of the nation were put under state control, all the profit which now goes into the hands of a few idle men, would go into the coffers of the state—which means that the people would enjoy the benefits of all the wealth they create.

"This, then, is the basis of socialism, that England should be owned by the English, and managed for the benefit of the English, instead of being owned by a few rich idlers, and mismanaged by them for the benefit of themselves." And a little further on : "Why nationalise the land and instruments of production? To save waste; to save panics; to avert trade depressions, famines, strikes ... In short, to replace anarchy and war by law and order."

Working-class candidates were beginning to get into Parliament. The two miners had been elected in 1874; by 1885 there were eleven working-class MPs. Most of these members sat with the Liberals, and were commonly referred to by the term "Lib-Lab". But in 1893 a new direction was taken by the working-class movement—the establishment of an independent political party. At a meeting in Bradford— of representatives of Labour groups and socialist societies largely from the North of England and Scotland—the Independent Labour Party was founded with Keir Hardie as chairman. SDF and Fabians were represented, but neither body was prepared to give up its own identity. Hardie had started work in the coal mines at the age of ten. He was a Scot, a religious man, of marked integrity, a straightforward man; he became a devoted leader of the workers' cause. He had been elected to the House of Commons in 1892 (as an independent Labour representative) and appeared in his miner's cap and rough tweed suit; he was conspicuous among the top hats and frock coats which members wore in those days, but eventually he won respect. The title of his new organisation reflected its origin in northern local groups which were feeling their way towards independence, and also perhaps a wish to avoid controversy which might be aroused by using the term socialist. But the organisation had a definite socialist character from the beginning: almost unanimously a motion was carried in favour of "the collective ownership of the means of production, distribution and exchange"; and, in a programme (dated a few years later), the socialist aim was again clearly stated: "The object of the Party is to establish the Socialist State, when land and capital will be held by the community, and when the exchange of commodities will be organised also by the community, so as to secure the highest possible standard of life for the individual. In giving effect to this object it shall work as part of the International Socialist movement". At first the ILP made no headway in winning elections, but it did have considerable influence on local activists in the trade unions, who in time had their effect on union policy. Hardie came to see that he must gain the support of the trade unions with their big membership and large funds before a Labour Party could become a practical proposition. Bernard Shaw, on behalf of the Fabians, had put forward a plan in 1894 for fifty Labour candidates to be financed by the unions. And it had not necessarily proved easy to win the support of the unions for a socialist policy—many, notably the miners, supported the Liberal Party. Working men had a practical outlook, had a material stake in the efficient working of the existing system, were not intellectuals, and were inclined to dislike mere theories.

Indeed the bringing together of socialist theory and the powerful numerical strength of the trade unions was the master stroke of the socialists. But it did not happen all at once; it was, in fact, not so much a stroke as a process. The close association of the trade unions and the Labour Party came to be taken for granted once the Labour Party was established, but it had not always been the case. The Webbs, in their *Industrial Democracy* published in 1897, had pointed out that the Trades Union Congress if it departed from its narrow trade union function and expressed opinions on general social and political questions would antagonise its members. This would happen because, as they said, "the trade unionists of Northumberland and Durham are predominantly Liberal. Those of Lancashire are largely Conservative. Those of Yorkshire and London, again, are deeply impregnated with Socialism." As early as 1892 Hardie was working in the TUC for independent labour representation, but many were against him and he made but little headway. English trade unionists were conservative in attitude, clinging to their older allegiance—most of the leaders were Gladstonian Liberals. And the miners—living in mining areas populated with their own people—could get their candidates elected easily enough without the support of any labour organisation. So it was that the card vote at the TUC of 1899 which led to the initiation of an independent labour organisation (the Labour Representation Committee) was a close thing : 546,000 in favour, 434,000 against. But once made, the decision proved a momentous one. Trade union affiliated membership of the Labour Party increased from some 350,000 members in 1900 to a little under two million in 1912 (the Miners' Federation having come over in 1910) —partly because the unions felt themselves threatened by legal decisions, the Taff Vale case involving liability for damages caused by strike action and the Osborne judgement threatening their use of union funds for political purposes. Though Liberal legislation removed the threat, the result was that Labour Party strength came to rest firmly on the mass trade union vote and the financial help of union funds. With the decision of 1899 things moved more rapidly.

In 1900 a meeting was arranged in London between representatives of the ILP, the Fabians, the old SDF, and the trade unions. At this meeting they all agreed to support a Labour Representation Committee (with Ramsay Mac-Donald as secretary), and in the same year, two of its candidates, of whom Hardie was one, were elected to Parliament. But this new Labour organisation was not yet avowedly socialist. In 1906 the LRC became the Labour Party, when twenty-nine of its members were elected to Parliament in the general election of that year. Among them were Ramsay MacDonald and Philip Snowden, who were, eighteen years later, to be Prime Minister and Chancellor of the Exchequer in the first Labour Government ever formed in the United Kingdom. Almost by the back door, socialism crept in as a party policy. Such were the beginnings of the Labour Party, which, though small at first, would after the First World War replace the Liberal Party as the second of the two great parties in the state.

But before then there would be many difficult passages. During the years immediately preceding the First World War politics were marked by a new violence: the trade unions turned to direct action, the suffragettes mounted a campaign of violent demonstration and disturbance, and in Ireland there was the threat of civil war. A wave of strikes in 1910, 1911, and 1912—some in spite of union advice to the contrary—led to serious outbreaks: rioting at Tony-pandy in South Wales, and trouble in Liverpool and Llanelly, in both of which troops opened fire and men were killed. And neither the Labour Party nor the form of socialist theory was yet securely established.

Victor Grayson caused something of a sensation in 1907 by winning Colne Valley without official Labour support, putting himself forward as an independent socialist. He challenged the Labour Party in the House of Commons, and the outcome of his disruptive tactics was the formation in 1911 of a new group, the British Socialist Party. But its effect was small. Grayson lost his seat in 1910 and, after the war, mysteriously disappeared. Another important challenge came from supporters of "Direct Action", the Syndicalists, who were influenced by the ideas of French Syndicalism and the International Workers of the World of America. The new movement of industrial unionism rejected parliamentary party methods and the older bureaucratic leadership of the trade unions; it represented a militant unionism, advocating the taking over of industry by the workers themselves. Leader of the movement was Tom Mann, who had led the great Dock Strike of 1889. In South Wales the miners put forward their syndicalist programme in 1912—*The Miners' Next Step.* "The mines for the miners" was the slogan : the state as well as the employer was to be fought, and by revolutionary action through strike after strike, the miners were to bring the coalfields under working class control.

Another threat to the idea of state socialism came from what was known as Guild Socialism. Some of the Guild Socialists supported Victor Grayson. Guild Socialists looked back to Ruskin and the guilds of the Middle Ages, and aimed at abolishing the wage system and establishing self-government in industry through national guilds. Prominent in this movement were A. R. Orage and G. D. H. Cole. In 1916 Cole contributed an article on Guild Socialism to the *Labour Year Book*—an official party publication—and this suggests that party policy as to public ownership was still flexible. Guild Socialist and Syndicalist ideas were influential for a time, a number of builders' guilds were set up after the war though they were short-lived. But the ideas did not become predominant, and the principle of state socialism eventually reasserted itself.

6. The Ideas of British Socialism

K ARL MARX HAD waited in vain for the expected revolution, but soon after his death the Fabian Society, founded in 1884, began to make its distinctive contribution to the development of socialism in this country—a gradualist or evolutionary, rather than a revolutionary, approach. This is, broadly speaking, how one can conveniently distinguish the two main attitudes to socialist strategy; at the same time, one cannot always find them so clearly distinguished at any given moment. E. R. Pease, the secretary of the Society and its historian, maintained that it was from the start against the revolutionary policy of the SDF, whereas Bernard Shaw did not remember it as marked out, at first, in this way. But a little later Shaw came to see that as a practical policy the Fabian way was to be preferred to the revolutionary. It was Frank Podmore (afterwards the biographer of Robert Owen) who suggested the name "Fabian", explaining, according to Pease, "For the right moment you must wait, as Fabius did most patiently when warring against Hannibal, though many censured his delays : but when the time comes you must strike hard, as Fabius did, or your waiting will be in vain and fruitless". And "when the time comes you must strike hard" could be taken as equivalent to revolution. Individual members doubtless had their own views, or put their own interpretations on the views of others. But as time went on the two attitudes could be more easily distinguished —the Fabians as gradualists, the Marxists as revolutionaries.

Individual members might change their views, or modify them, and the many groups and organisations springing up, often of a transient kind, and the changes of name or description—all this shows the constant flux in the socialist movement and the impossibility of precise definition. As with the attitude to revolution, so with the attitude to Marx in general, the Fabians could not wholeheartedly accept the lead which had been given by the Marxist Hyndman, yet "whilst not entirely agreeing with the statements and phrases used in the pamphlets of the Democratic Federation, and in the speeches of Mr Hyndman", the Society considered that the Federation "is doing good and useful work and is worthy of sympathy and support". William Morris, who followed the Marx-Hyndman line on revolution—though Marx had disowned Hyndman, and Morris split with Hyndman and was in touch with Engels when the Socialist League was formed as against the SDF—William Morris could also belong to the Fabians and take a very cavalier attitude to Marx's economics. "Does Comrade Morris accept Marx's theory of value?" a supporter of Hyndman asked him at a meeting. "To speak frankly, I do not know what Marx's theory of value is," Morris answered, "and I'm damned if I want to know . . . . It is enough political economy for me to know that the idle rich class is rich and the working class is poor, and that the rich are rich because they rob the poor." And so it seems that Morris took a short cut to Marx's theory of surplus value by the light of nature rather than by any profound study of the master. Beatrice Potter (who worked for her relative, Charles Booth, on his *Life and Labour of the People of London*, and was later Mrs. Webb) and Bernard Shaw took Marx more seriously. The former experienced a certain elation in her Marxian studies, and reminded herself when depressed that "Constant intellectual endeavour is the only safeguard against morbid feeling". But she found that she could not accept Marx's theory of value. In what she called "the weird Marxian World" the demand side, the part of the consumer in creating value by his demand for the goods provided by labour, was ignored. "To read Marx," she wrote, "one would think that it was only necessary to make a yard of cloth in order to create exchange value equal to the cost of production, together with a handsome surplus!" Bernard Shaw, at first convinced by Marx, found a little later he must abandon the theory of value. What happened, as described by Shaw, well illustrates the variety of social rostrums at the time and how the earnest seeker after truth tried one after the other. Shaw heard Henry George (whose *Progress and Poverty*, 1879, advocated a tax on land as the remedy for all social ills) speak in London in 1884. As a result Shaw turned from agnostic controversies to economics, and attended a meeting of

Hyndman's Democratic Federation. There he was contemptuously dismissed as a novice because he had not read Marx's *Capital*, which he thereupon sought out (in the French version) in the British Museum reading room. Impressed at first and entering into controversy in a periodical, Shaw was at length convinced that the Marxian theory of value was unsatisfactory. After these intellectual comings and goings Shaw joined the Fabians, and was—eventually—their most illustrious member.

The Fabian Society originated quite humbly, but was to prove one of the longest-lived of socialist societies. In October 1883, a little group, of some sixteen persons, met in the rooms of E. R. Pease, then a young man engaged in business but at the same time an admirer of William Morris, and they met to hear a paper on "The New Life". After further discussions, a Fellowship of the New Life was planned with the object : "the cultivation of a perfect character in each and all". This, to some, seemed a little sweeping and a little vague, and at a meeting in January 1884, the members split. The majority founded the Fabian Society with the aim of the reconstruction of society (although the minority carried on for some years with their Fellowship), set up an executive committee, and began to arrange lectures and the publication of pamphlets—Rosamund Dale Owen, grand-daughter of Robert Owen, was a member of the pamphlet committee. In 1887 a "Basis" was drawn up to which members must subscribe—it stated briefly the socialist aim, and that it was to be achieved by a general dissemination of knowledge and the spread of socialist opinions. But with only about twenty members—and only one from the working class—there was no reason at first to see in the society anything more than could have been seen in many another small socialistic group. Then, later in the year, Bernard Shaw joined, and next year brought his friend Sidney Webb, a clerk in the Colonial Office; next came Sydney Olivier (later Lord Olivier), also in the Colonial

Office, Graham Wallas, afterwards a professor at the London School of Economics, and Annie Besant, a well-known speaker in the cause of secularism. At the time these names—except that of Mrs Besant—were unknown. They would win fame in the future, and with it influence for the Society. Membership grew—and it was distinguished—and societies were founded in a number of cities.

The Fabians were at first a somewhat restricted and select group—applicants for membership had to be proposed and seconded—and it may be that they were influenced by a feeling of intellectual superiority; they were middle class, and met on terms of something like financial and educational equality. Shaw tells of the meetings in one another's drawing rooms, and of the habit which members developed of freely laughing at each other—all of which suggests rather an élitist clique. It is curious, too, that H. G. Wells, though twenty years later, remarked on the irritating tendency of members to have their private jokes and to giggle at them. Was there, perhaps, too much of the social scientist—looking at human beings and their doings as something to be organised, arranged, put right? Beatrice Potter wrote in her diary of East End life—"Where is the wish for better things in these myriads of beings hurrying along the streets night and day?" Some people felt that they were regarded by the Webbs as a means to the Webbs' end, not as ends in themselves. There was something more attractive in the bluff socialism of Charles Kingsley and Thomas Hughes, or in the cheerful good sense of Robert Blatchford, or in the working class fervour of Keir Hardie. Yet, in their time, the Fabians did a great work of socialist propaganda and preparation, in lecturing and speaking, in writing tracts and studying reports and statistics, and in getting elected to and working on local government bodies. Their especial contribution was to put their advocacy of socialism on a basis, not of emotion, but of reason and information. An early tract, *Facts for*

Socialists, was backed by the belief that any sensible person, once he knew the facts, would become a socialist.

Fabian Essays in Socialism was the Society's most striking and successful effort. Published in 1889, it was based on lectures given by the Fabians in the previous year in London and the provinces; and the Fabian lectures in London became an annual event. The book was edited by Bernard Shaw; it was an immediate success, and went on selling for many years. It gave a clear, short, comprehensive view of socialism, based on the authors' "common conviction of the necessity of vesting the organisation of industry and the material of production in a State identified with the whole people by complete Democracy". There were eight essays, divided into three sections. On "The Basis of Socialism" Bernard Shaw wrote on the Economic, Sidney Webb on the Historic, William Clarke on the Industrial, and Sydney Olivier on the Moral basis; on "The Organisation of Society" Graham Wallas dealt with Property under Socialism, and Annie Besant with Industry under Socialism; and in the final section "The Transition to Social Democracy" Bernard Shaw contributed Transition, and Hubert Bland a closing essay, The Outlook.

Bernard Shaw with his incomparable style, lightness of touch, and humorous treatment could appeal both to reader and listener. He starts, as he says all economic analysis must, with the cultivation of the earth. One man sticks in his spade and, with heavy toil, produces maybe an indifferent crop; another finds gold, or coal, or taps a jet of petroleum. Thus man is mocked—he never knows whether the earth will give him diamonds or blighted cabbages. He becomes a gambler—yet he rebels against his fate. He knows that in gambling the many lose in order that the few may win. He desires that the capricious gifts of nature may be intercepted by some power having the goodwill to distribute them justly so that each worker will be rewarded according to the amount of labour he puts into the collective effort to find or produce what nature offers. "This desire is socialism." He then goes on to follow the orthodox economists—with references to their works—in showing how an empty unsettled country is settled by private property. The firstcomer —"the original Adam, developed by centuries of civilisation into an Adam Smith"—prospects for a suitable patch of private property; as the economists assume, he is "on the make" and settles on the best land he can find. Others come, and all the good land is settled. Those who come later still must work poorer land, getting a poorer return than the firstcomers who occupied the better land. The holders of the best land are now in a strong position; they can retire from manual work, and rent their land—or some of it—to tenants, the tenants paying a rent equal to the difference between the product of the best land and that of the poorest land which is just worth cultivating. In this way landed families are founded, with tenants and sub-tenants to work for them. But at length the proletarian arrives—the man with nothing, and who can acquire no land because the country is already fully settled. What is he to do? "He has nothing to sell— except himself." So he sells his labour to the tenant cultivators—"labour power is now in the market on the same footing as any other ware exposed there for sale".

Shaw goes on to deal with exchange and value. He shows, like the orthodox economists, that exchange arises as soon as men give up providing each one by his own labour for all their needs. Division of labour develops, and the man who sticks to making tables and chairs will exchange what he does not need himself for other things such as bread and clothes. He will find that his articles have an exchange value, which, for convenience, comes to be expressed in gold or money. But there is a difficulty about what actually fixes exchange value. Clearly it must depend on utility—something which is useless will not exchange. Yet air and sunlight are useful, indispensable, and nevertheless have no exchange value. This is because they are plentiful; and what has exchange value is limited, the more limited the more valuable. The marginal theory of value is now expounded—"exchange value is fixed by the utility, not of the most useful, but of the least useful part of the stock", that part which is just worth while producing, and is on the margin of production. Shaw saw clearly that if a producer "produces a useless thing, his labour will be wholly vain : he will get nothing for it. If he produces a useful thing, the price he will get for it will depend on how much of it there is for sale already" and "man's control over the value of commodities consists solely in his power of regulating their supply". Hence conspiracies to forestall the world's wheat or cotton harvests, hence the destruction of cargoes of fish to maintain price, hence all trusts, corners in the market, monopolies.

This brings him back to the proletarian and "the latent horror" of his situation. He has little or no control over the supply of labour power. Indeed his natural instinct leads him irresistibly to increase it. The increase in numbers of the proletariat forces their exchange value down and down "until it disappears altogether". This has happened already in England, he maintains : the workers "are no longer even dirt cheap: they are valueless, and can be had for nothing. The proof is the existence of the unemployed, who can find no purchasers". What then of those who are employed and paid wages? Their wage is only their keep. "For bare subsistence wages you can get as much common labour as you want." Capitalism then, is merely providing provender for the necessary labour force. "If a railway is required, all that is necessary is to provide subsistence for a sufficient number of labourers to construct it. . . . This subsistence is technically called capital. It is provided for by the proprietors not consuming the whole excess over wages of the produce of the labour of their other wage workers, but setting aside enough for the subsistence of the railway workers." Next comes a suggestion that the capitalist system leads to the rapid multiplication in numbers of the working classes. The cry is heard of over-population—"but your slaves are beyond caring for your cries : they breed like rabbits; and their poverty breeds filth, ugliness, dishonesty, disease, obscenity, drunkenness, and murder"; and here a Marxist touch—"In the midst of the riches which their labour piles up for you, their misery rises up too and stifles you . . . then comes the terror of their revolting . . . paroxysms of frantic coercion, followed by paroxysms of frantic charity", summed up by Shaw as "this grotesquely hideous march of civilisation from bad to worse".

This economic analysis, he maintains, shows that the system of private property is quite unable to solve the problem "of adjusting the share of the worker in the distribution of wealth to the labour incurred by him in its production". Old civilisations have disappeared because they failed to solve the problem, they rotted into centres of vice and luxury. He admits the safety valve of emigration, and a degree of restitution to the workers through the income tax, provision of education, and factory legislation. He admits, too, that his analysis has been over-simplified, that property in Europe did not originate exactly as suggested. On the whole, however, "history, even in the Old World, goes the way traced by the economist". But socialism offers a solution of the economic problem. This solution is to transfer to the incomes of the workers those incomes, that is rent and interest, which are derived from private property—for these incomes from private property are "paid out of the difference between the produce of the worker's labour and the price of that labour sold in the open market for wages, salary, fees, or profits". In this Shaw has come back to Marx, which he recognises himself in a footnote—"This excess of the product of labour over its price is treated as a single category with impressive effect by Karl Marx, who called it 'surplus value' ".

And so Shaw offered his analysis and his solution to the good sense and the good will of his readers. He thought that a terrible burden would be lifted from their minds. It had been terrible to see the poverty of the people and yet to fear that it could not be helped—"that the poor must starve and make you ashamed of your dinner". But now "economic science—once the dismal, now the hopeful"—shows that the social evil is not eternal but can be removed when people are convinced and bestir themselves to make an end of it.

Sidney Webb, like Shaw, also made socialism seem something quite natural, acceptable, and to be expected in the due course of events. Dealing with the historic basis of socialism, he showed how the unrestrained individualism and private property of the early nineteenth century had already had to be limited and regulated by the state, and that, indeed "the economic history of the century is an almost continuous record of the progress of socialism". The old socialist ideas—of Plato, More, Robert Owen—had pictured a static condition. But now—thanks to Comte, Darwin, and Herbert Spencer—we look for "the gradual evolution of the new order from the old, without breach of continuity or abrupt change of the entire social tissue at any point during the process . . . and history shows us no example of the sudden substitutions of Utopian and revolutionary romance". Democracy has been the main stream carrying society towards socialism, and it means "that it is through the slow and gradual turning of the popular mind to new principles that social reorganisation bit by bit comes". Thus important changes must be acceptable to the people, gradual, causing no dislocation, and, in this country at any rate, constitutional and peaceful. Radicals, as well as socialists, he maintains, are coming to see that there must be "the gradual substitution of organised co-operation for the anarchy of the competitive struggle". Webb then takes the reader through the main social changes: from the decay of feudalism through the Industrial Revolution and the French Revolution,

through the period of *Laisser-faire* and anarchic individualism with the subsequent intellectual and moral revolt
against it (Robert Owen, Carlyle, the Christian Socialists,
J. S. Mill, etc.), to the recent extension of state and municipal
activity, of which he gives a surprisingly lengthy list—among
others, factory acts, health acts, the post office (the largest
employer of labour), the armed services, the coinage, roads,
and municipal gas, water, and tramways. He also points out
that, whereas the older economists had supposed that industry must be carried on by personal management, all
kinds of industry were now being carried on by joint stock
companies employing salaried officers, and their "shareholders could be expropriated by the community with no
more dislocation of the industries carried on by them than
is caused by the daily purchase of shares on the Stock
Exchange". So the moral was that socialism was well on
the way already. Its realisation was part of the social evolution, of "our irresistible glide into collectivist socialism". "If
private property in land and capital necessarily keeps the
many workers poor (through no fault of their own) in order
to make the few idlers rich (from no merit of their own),
private property in land and capital will inevitably go the
way of the feudalism which it superseded". And yet—"inevitably" (as also with the *Communist Manifesto*) did not
remove the necessity of individual and party action. "The
Zeitgeist is potent; but it does not pass acts of parliament
without legislators.... It still rests with the individual to
resist or promote the social evolution."

To summarise the main principles of the *Essays*, taken
together, one would notice in particular the following. They
recognised the transformation of society by industry—they
went some of the way with Marx's materialist conception of
history here—and they saw (particularly William Clarke on
the Industrial basis of socialism) that the socialists' task is
not to undo what the capitalists had created, but to take
over or control, by one means or another, the capitalist

undertakings and use them in the public interest. They saw this being done gradually, democratically, by means of parliament and local government, in a step by step extension of public control over productive enterprises and public services. They saw that socialised industries could be run by salaried managers, and at first would have to compete for them with private industry. They were not yet clearly committed to nationalisation, although later they moved far in this direction. "The inevitability of gradualness" was formulated clearly in Webb's essay, and he used the phrase itself over thirty years later in his presidential address to the Labour Party Conference in 1923. Shaw accepted this view —but with a typically Shavian twist he tried to make the best of both worlds, the revolutionary and the gradualist. In his second essay, his flamboyant nature could not deny itself a reference to the enthusiasm of revolutionary socialism. Of revolution, he concluded: "The proposal proved impracticable; and it has now been abandoned—not without some outspoken regrets—by English socialists. But it still remains as the only finally possible alternative to the Social Democratic programme which I have sketched today."

When Beatrice Potter read a copy of *Fabian Essays*— before she was engaged to Webb—she remarked that "by far the most significant and interesting essay is the one by Sidney Webb". That opinion might be challenged, for Bernard Shaw's contributions were outstanding in their ability to present socialism in popular form. Webb and Shaw made a most effective partnership. Webb was remarkable as an assiduous worker and organiser (and also as a member of the London County Council), and Shaw spoke of the generalship of the movement being undertaken largely by him. The Fabians urged their members to permeate the other parties, to join their local Liberal, or even Conservative, associations, to make speeches and move resolutions; they put many ideas into the heads of the Progressives in London who gained a majority in the first London County

Council; they gained a foothold in the press. "We pulled all the wires we could lay our hands on," said Shaw, "with our utmost adroitness and energy." And what wires the Fabian had to pull! Beatrice Potter tells of a party in 1891 at the house of her friend Mrs J. R. Green. Five of the Liberals—Asquith, Haldane, Grey, Buxton, and Acland— were there to meet five Fabians—Webb, Shaw, Olivier, Clarke and Massingham. The meeting did not go well— Asquith, apparently, was determined it should not. But the very fact of the meeting is indicative of the influence of the Fabians and of their calibre. All the Liberals became cabinet ministers, and Asquith prime minister; two of the Fabians (Webb and Olivier) and one of the Liberals (Haldane) were members of the first Labour cabinet, and Bernard Shaw became as dramatist and socialist most famous of all.

7. The Lives of the Socialists

THE LIVES OF the working class pioneers of socialism were very different from those of the middle-class and well-to-do Fabians. Keir Hardie was born in 1856 in a one-roomed tumbledown cottage in a Lanarkshire village, started work as a messenger at seven years of age, and went down the pit at ten to sit all day in the dark to open and shut a door which circulated air to the miners. He did not often see daylight during the winter months. It was not, therefore, mere coincidence that there was sometimes a certain friction between the Fabians and the ILP. There was in any case the natural suspicion of and rivalry with another socialist group—the SDF over again as it appeared. But the dislike seemed rather more personal on the part of Beatrice Webb and Shaw; the latter is reported to have said in a letter to Sidney Webb: "My estimate of K.H. is that he is a Scotchman with alternate intervals of second sight (during which he does not see anything, but is suffused with afflatus) and common incapacity." But the difference was deep: for the Fabians socialism was an intellectual interest, for the working class a matter of life and death; for the Fabians men were units to be schooled, trained, organised, socialised; for Hardie man, however humble, was an individual with a dignity of his own. As Ramsay MacDonald wrote of Hardie: "... his socialism was not an economic doctrine, not a formula.... He got more socialism from Burns than from Marx; *The Twa Dogs* and *A Man's a Man for a' that* were more prolific textbooks for his politics than *Das Kapital*." Yet Fabian Society and ILP were complementary. As G. D. H. Cole put it: 'Hardie and the ILP were a genuine and influential movement lacking a clear or constructive policy; the Fabians were a group of highly intelligent leaders lacking a rank and file. They helped and mutually formed each other."

An illegitimate son, James Keir Hardie's origins were both humble and obscure. His father was a miner, his mother a farm servant, Mary Keir, who afterwards married a ship's carpenter, David Hardie. They left the village, and went to live near the shipyards. Poverty was the family's lot, especially as it grew in numbers, and as an accident and unemployment struck its head. His mother and David Hardie taught the young James to read. He attended a night school, where there was a good teacher but no light provided; each pupil had to bring his own candle. The parents were thinking people of independent outlook; they did not go to church, and were hostile to religion. The boy soon developed a love of reading, began to look out on the world around him, and to think for himself.

One incident stood out in his childhood, while the family was in Glasgow, and Hardie left his own description of it. It was "not only a turning point in my life, but also in my outlook upon men and things". The prospect was black in the

family : one brother was ill and soon to die, there was another child on the way, and there was no work, James being
the only member of the family with a job. "One winter
morning I turned up late at the baker's shop where I was
employed and was told I had to go upstairs to see the master.
I was kept waiting outside the door of the dining-room while
he said grace—he was noted for religious zeal—and, on being
admitted, found the master and his family seated round a
large table. He was serving out bacon and eggs while the
wife was pouring coffee. . . . I had never before seen such a
beautiful room, nor such a table, loaded as it was with
food. . . ." He was warned that, if late again, he would be
dismissed. "The injustice of the thing was burning hot within
me, all the more that I could not explain why I was late. The
fact was that I had not yet tasted food. I had been up most
of the night tending my ailing brother, and had risen betimes
in the morning but had been made late by assisting my
mother in various ways before starting." Then, two days
afterwards, he was again a few minutes late; he was told that
he was discharged, and his fortnight's wages were forfeited
as punishment. "The news stupefied me, and finally I burst
out crying. . . . The morning was wet and I had been
drenched in getting to the shop, and must have presented a
pitiable sight as I stood at the counter in my wet patched
clothes. . . . For a time I wandered about the streets in the
rain, ashamed to go home where there was neither food nor
fire, and actually discussing whether the best thing was not
to go and throw myself in the Clyde and be done with a life
that had so little attractions. In the end I went to the shop
and saw the master and explained why I had been late. But
it was all in vain. The wages were never paid. But the master
continued to be a pillar of the church and a leading light in
the religious life of the city."

Soon after this the father went back to the sea, and the
mother and her family removed to the mining community
where her own mother was still living. It was now that James

started in the mines as a trapper. By the time he was twenty
he was thoroughly experienced as a miner. But his earnest
and serious character led him to seek some form of useful
service to his fellow men. He worked for the temperance
movement, and to the surprise of the family he started going
to church. He found in the Evangelical Union a simple form
of Christianity. These activities brought him into the miners'
affairs; he took the chair at meetings, and went on deputa-
tions to the colliery managers. He became known as an agitator, and was dismissed, the dismissal including his two
younger brothers. "We'll hae nae damned Hardies in this
pit," said the manager. The miners in Lanarkshire were dis-
organised, and a leader was needed. Hardie threw himself
into the struggle; he and his mother supported themselves by
keeping small shops, and the young man started writing and
reporting for the local papers. At the age of twenty-three, he
was elected miners' agent. By this time he was a Christian
and something of a socialist. During the next few years Hardie
was occupied in organising the miners, first in Lanarkshire,
then in Ayrshire—there were strikes, and the miners' brass
bands marched through the villages—and finally in making
the beginnings of a Scottish national miners' federation. At
first, in politics, Hardie supported the Liberals. He maintained himself by his newspaper and union work, he was still
active in the temperance movement and the Evangelical
Union, and from time to time he preached in the chapels. But
he came more and more to question whether the Liberal
Party could truly represent the working class. Liberal candidates, like the Conservative candidates, were usually selected
by the organisations, in which wealthy people were influential, and were sent to the constituencies. Hardie thought the
working people should have a voice in their selection, and
that Labour men, independent of the two existing parties,
were needed to represent the working class. It was not so
much socialism which moved Hardie as the ideal of Christian
brotherhood. As he put it : "The world today is sick and

weary at heart. Even our clergy are for the most part dumb dogs who dare not bark. So it was in the days of Christ. They who proclaimed a God-given gospel to the world were the poor and the comparatively unlettered. We need today a return to the principles of that Gospel which, by proclaiming all men sons of God and brethren one with another, makes it impossible for one, Shylock-like, to insist on his rights at the expense of another."

This was the spirit of Keir Hardie. In this spirit he spent his life in ceaseless work for the unions, the co-operative movement, the Labour movement as a whole, as MP first for West Ham, then for the last fifteen years of his life (1900-15) for Merthyr in South Wales, as chairman of the ILP, and then as chairman of the Parliamentary Labour Party. He was known abroad also—on a world tour, on visits to America, and at international socialist conferences. He thought that the common sense of socialism would appear everywhere; few would be scientific economists, but all are human. "Socialism," he said, "means fraternity founded on justice, and the fact that in order to secure this it is necessary to transfer land and capital from private to public ownership is a mere incident in the crusade." Standing for the independence of Labour, he resisted every attempt at patronage or at winning him over, by the Liberals or by the employers. He was incorruptible. Long after his death it was remembered in South Wales how, when at meetings of the miners and the owners, the latter, to oil the wheels of negotiation, would give the men's leaders a pound or two for a night out, Hardie would take nothing. He might be described as a saint of the Labour movement. Trade union friends recalled a meeting at Norwich when, one evening in the cathedral grounds, the voice of Hardie was suddenly heard singing the Twenty-third Psalm—and all present joined in. In 1901, when he secured a place in the private members' ballot, he had the opportunity to introduce a socialist resolution in the House of Commons, asking for legislation to inaugurate "a Socialist Commonwealth founded upon the common ownership of land and capital, production for use and not for profit, and equality of opportunity for every citizen". In about twenty minutes before midnight, he presented his case. "We are called upon," he said in his closing words, "to decide the question propounded in the Sermon on the Mount, as to whether we will worship God or Mammon. The last has not been heard of this movement either in the House or in the country, for as surely as Radicalism democratised the system of government politically in the last century, so will Socialism democratise the industrialism of the country in the coming century."

But amid the theoretical patterns of political and economic development the inconstancy of human nature remained a constant factor. For with Ramsay MacDonald as with Keir Hardie the Scottish lament of the miller's daughter of Allan Water repeated itself. The love affair of John MacDonald, the ploughman from the Black Isle, with Anne Ramsay, the young housekeeper at a farm near Elgin, was short. Anne returned to Lossiemouth to her mother, whose own husband had abandoned her when Anne and her sisters and brothers were small children. Anne's child, James Ramsay Mac-Donald, was born in 1866 in a but-and-ben cottage in Lossie-mouth, and, without a father, was brought up by his mother and grandmother. They were poor, but cheerful and hard working. James went to school, and got a solid education— as was common in Scottish village schools, the schoolmaster would give extra time to the more intelligent boys, and so James went on to a grounding in Latin and Greek.

And at home also there was education. There were books in the cottage—the Bible, a *Life of Christ*, a few religious books, one or two of the classics in their original, *Pilgrim's Progress*, the poems of Burns. He was influenced by the life stories, then not long published, of three notable Scotsmen, like himself humbly born and having to struggle for their education. Hugh Miller's *My Schools and Schoolmasters* told the story of the Cromarty stonemason, his search for knowledge, and his study of the rocks. This and Samuel Smiles' *Life of a Scottish Naturalist, Thomas Edward* and his *Robert Dick, Baker of Thurso, Geologist and Botanist*—together with Orr's *Circle of the Sciences*—introduced him to the world of science. The Thurso baker was an extraordinary self-educated amateur who in pursuit of knowledge walked the thirty miles from Thurso to the summit of Morven, and back, and got up next morning to bake the bread. Cassell's *Popular Educator* MacDonald found most useful—his university, he called it later. He read Scott's *Tales of a Grandfather*, and Dickens, volume by volume, lent to him by a watchmaker in Lossiemouth. When he was about sixteen the schoolmaster took him on as a pupil teacher. His intellectual horizon widened; he got some socialistic ideas from Carlyle and Ruskin, and Henry George's *Progress and Poverty*. But at that time he was for Gladstone and Liberalism. He was speaking and debating in the Lossiemouth Mutual Improvement Association; he was active in a Lossiemouth Field Club, and in producing a Field Club magazine. There was, too, the intense religious life of a Scottish village, with its Sunday services and its prayer-meetings during the week.

It was chance—a newspaper advertisement of a job—which brought him to Bristol in 1885, to work with a clergyman in running a Boys' and Young Men's Guild, and in Bristol there happened to be a branch of the SDF. The young MacDonald heard of the socialist group, sought it out, and joined—he read them a paper on Ruskin. He was active in its affairs—in forming a small collection of books and in holding out-of-door meetings; and the future prime minister made his first speech, so it was said later, to an audience of three. But his job in Bristol came to an end, and he had, with his high hopes disappointed, to return to Lossiemouth.

But the next year the chance of another job took him to London. He found, however, that the post was already filled, and he tramped the streets looking for work. It was a somewhat desperate time, while he lived on next to nothing. He found something, and there followed a number of temporary clerical jobs, with a breakdown in health and another short return to Lossiemouth. At length, in 1888, an opportunity came his way. He became a private secretary to a Liberal candidate, and this event was the turning point in his career; it gave him a small salary, a small security, and contacts, particularly contacts with men in the world of politics and journalism. Now at last his personality and natural ability could make themselves felt. During these years in London MacDonald was in touch with all the socialist groups —with the Fabians (whom he joined in 1886), with the Fellowship of the New Life (he acted as unpaid secretary in 1892) from which the Fabian Society had originated, with the SDF. From 1894 to 1900 MacDonald was a member of the executive of the Fabian Society. He got to know the Fabian leaders, and for a time he had a room in a house shared by a number of Fabians and New Life Fellowship people—a kind of community settlement. He was in touch with Keir Hardie, and joined the ILP in 1894. In joining the new independent socialist organisation and abandoning the Liberal Party MacDonald was influenced by what seemed the unreasonable reluctance of local Liberal Associations to accept working class candidates. There had been a proposal to put up MacDonald as a candidate at Southampton, but the negotiations broke down; at Attercliffe, shortly afterwards, the Liberals would not accept a trade union candidate. For the young MacDonald this was the parting of the political ways. When he did stand for Southampton (though unsuccessfully) in the following year—as an ILP Candidate —he disclosed in his election manifesto: "I ceased to trust in the Liberal Party when I was convinced that they were not prepared to go on and courageously face the bread-and-butter problems of the time—the problems of poverty, stunted lives, and pauper-and-criminal-making conditions of labour. Neither Tories nor Liberals have a Labour policy as we understand it." And he went on to plead for nationalisation of the land, the railways, and mining royalties—and for the "public control of the means of production, distribution and exchange". But MacDonald's socialist thinking was very much along the lines of the Fabian, evolutionary approach. His scientific, particularly his biological interest, led him to regard Marx as unscientific. Some years later, his *Socialism and Society* (published in 1905), developed this attitude. "The Hegelian dialectic is unfitted to describe biological evolution," he wrote. Evolution, not revolution, was the natural development. "Socialism is inevitable, not because capitalism is to break down," he maintained, "but because man is a reasonable being."

By now MacDonald had a certain meagre independence, which his secretaryship, his writing for the newspapers, and his lecturing for the Fabians gave him. He went on energetically continuing his own education, reading steadily, at home and in the British Museum Library.

At this time, too, he met his future wife, Margaret Gladstone, a daughter of a distinguished scientist and FRS and great-niece of Lord Kelvin. They became engaged on the steps of the British Museum in 1896, and were married in the same year. His marriage was another turning point in his career. Though it is difficult to believe, in view of his later career, that even alone Ramsay MacDonald would not have gone far, his marriage gave him solid advantages. His wife had an independent income, foreign travel became possible, and his wife made him not only a supremely happy home but one which was a social and political centre—although they lived simply enough and the Scottish husband made the family porridge. Economic independence meant also political independence; he was not dependent for his income on the trade unions. He went on steadily with his political work In 1899 he was adopted parliamentary candidate for Leicester, and, although defeated in 1900, he was elected as

Labour member in 1906. His mother in Lossiemouth was aroused in the night to hear the news. The man who was to be first Labour prime minister of Britain was fairly launched on his way.

Other socialist leaders who served under him in the first and second Labour governments had similar early struggles with poverty—Snowden, Henderson, Clynes and Thomas. Ernest Bevin born in 1881 and James Griffith born in 1890 rose to prominence with the Second World War, but like Hardie and MacDonald and so many others, they had a similar story in their youth. Ernest Bevin was born in a remote west Somerset village, close to Exmoor. His mother, who had a daughter and six sons of whom Ernest was the last, had described herself as a widow for several years before Ernest was born, and who Ernest's father was is not known. His mother had to call up all her courage for the struggle to support the family, working as a domestic servant in neighbouring houses. Ernest went to the Church school and the Wesleyan sunday school. Then, when he was eight, his mother died. The family was broken up; the older boys went to work on farms, and the daughter Mary and her husband took the young half-brother into their home. He continued his elementary school attendance until 1892, laying the foundations of reading, writing, and arithmetic. Apart from that he had to rely on himself. In spite of being a countryman by birth, he did not, apparently, like the farm jobs he took after leaving school, and early in 1894 he set out for Bristol, where one of his brothers was already employed. There he had a variety of jobs : he worked in a bakery and delivered loads of pies to the refreshment room in Temple Meads station, he was a conductor on the horse trams, and he was a driver for a mineral water manufacturer. Meanwhile Nonconformity gave him not only a serious character to life but a continual means of education. He joined a Baptist chapel, he became a Sunday school teacher, and he spoke at open-air evangelical meetings. He read and studied; at one time he thought of taking a theological course and becoming a minister. He also attended discussions, meetings of the Adult School Movement, and WEA, YMCA, and Education Committee classes.

Slowly his outlook changed; it became less religious, more social in character. He saw about him in Bristol the great contrast between poverty and wealth. Why was there such a contrast?—he began to ask himself. Why were the few rich, and the many poor? He began to attend socialist meetings. Bristol had its socialist groups (Ramsay MacDonald had been influenced by such a group as a young man in Bristol in 1885): SDF and ILP. There were evening meetings in Old Market, the Horsefair, on Clifton Downs. Ernest Bevin would speak at these meetings, and he now turned his talents as a speaker to working class politics rather than religion. In 1908 he became secretary (unpaid) to the Bristol Right-to-Work Committee which was advocating municipal schemes of work for the unemployed. In 1909 he stood—unsuccessfully—for the Council, and by now he was a socialist. In his election address, referring to the unemployment in Bristol, he said: "You will realise the chaos, misery and degradation brought upon us by the private ownership of the means of life. I claim that Socialism, which is the common ownership of those means, is the only solution of such evils." In the next year, he became, after negotiations between the dockers and the carters in the Bristol docks, chairman of a carters' branch of the Dockers' Union, and so commenced his career as a trade unionist which would lead him, many years later, to the post of Minister of Labour and, later still, to the Foreign Office.

The Welsh mining valleys, which have produced so many radicals and socialists, produced James Griffiths. Labour MP for Llanelly from 1936 onwards, he was in each Labour government from the end of the Second World War until his retirement in 1966 and was deputy leader of the Parliamentary Labour Party from 1956-59. Born in 1890 near

Ammanford, in Carmarthenshire, his boyhood was passed in Betws, where a village way of life and village crafts, now long vanished, still persisted though under the dominance of coal. His father—and grandfather—was the village blacksmith, and his mother was daughter of a handloom weaver. Her brothers each had his own loom; the Welsh flannel they wove was sold in the fairs of Carmarthen and Llandeilo, and the colliers' wives made it up into shirts and pants—it was best for absorbing the sweat. The smithy was a kind of village parliament, where eager discussion went on under the guidance of blacksmith Griffiths—whose heroes were still the Liberal leaders, Gladstone, Tom Ellis and Lloyd George. The young Jim Griffiths went to the local Board school and to the sunday school in the Welsh chapel. And at home there were a few books; his father had Bible commentaries and some religious works, and there were radical journals and nonconformist weeklies. His father intended that, after a year or two in the mine, he should train for the Congregational ministry, and so in 1904, at the age of thirteen he started work in the pit—like his brothers and most young men in the valleys.

That same year came the Welsh religious revival. As James Griffiths described it later, everything seemed to be different; services were held even down the mine, and their home was virtually turned into a chapel. The revival transformed life for a year or two, and then it seemed to fade out and leave a void—a void soon to be filled by another kind of revival. For the Welsh fervour and emotionalism, which had so far found its outlet in religion, was now beginning to pass into socialism. Several years after the revival the Rev. R. J. Campbell, minister of the City Temple, the cathedral of nonconformity, visited the neighbourhood and there also came "from Merthyr the socialist Scotsman who was causing a stir in the valleys". James Griffiths heard Campbell urge all Christians to help in creating a new social order based on Christian ethics and to break loose from the outworn doctrines of the

Liberal Party. Then, in the miners' hall in Gwaun Cae Gurwen he heard Keir Hardie—Campbell had looked like a seer, Keir Hardie seemed a prophet. He pictured the Labour movement as an attempt to enable the working class to realise itself, to stand on its own feet without support, either Liberal or Conservative. "From these meetings," James Griffiths has recalled, "we returned with a new religion to inspire us—a cause to which we could dedicate our lives, and a call to action to 'change all this'. . . . Within a week we had formed a branch of the ILP." The ILP appealed, more than other forms of socialism, to their religious idealism. "The ILP's socialist programme, which aimed at the collective ownership of the means of production through parliamentary action, was more in accord with our temperament than the SDF's class war." But the new Labour movement, in its independence, was a challenge to both Liberalism and nonconformity, hitherto united. It split the chapels. "Choose—Christ or Socialism" was a slogan to be heard. Liberalism and nonconformity both declined and lost their grip in industrial Wales. The new Labour movement took their place. And so James Griffiths was launched into socialism. He continued his education, meanwhile, by WEA evening classes in economics, and immediately after the war won a miners' scholarship to a Labour college in London. Then, as first a miners' agent, next a Labour Party agent, he made his way into the political world.

And what was true of Keir Hardie and Ramsay MacDonald, of Snowden, Henderson, Clynes and J. H. Thomas, of Bevin and Griffiths, and many more was the rise from poverty through the Labour Party to positions of influence and the finding of a guiding light in the idea of socialism.

PART III

8. The War and New Opportunity

THE OUTBREAK IN 1914 of the First World War
—known as the Great War until 1939 brought an even
greater—was a staggering blow to the Labour movement. It
shattered the carefully-fostered myth of the international
solidarity of the working classes, and in every country it
distracted thought and effort away from socialism towards
the immediate object of winning the war. Yet, paradoxically,
the coming of war marked the beginning of a new period of
opportunity for socialism. The many pressures and disasters
of the war on the Eastern Front led to the collapse of Russia
and the emergence of a Soviet socialist or communist state,
the sheer fact of whose establishment led to a new importance for socialist movements everywhere; the common sacrifices and the co-operation of all classes in Britain led to a
new spirit and a new possibility for the Labour Party; and
the split in the Liberal Party and its subsequent decline gave
the Labour Party its chance to take its place as the second
great party in the state.

It might be supposed that working class socialists, living
in their own circumscribed world of earning a living, trade
union politics, and economic theory, would know nothing of
foreign affairs and must naturally have been taken unawares

by the catastrophe of 1914. They were, though Keir Hardie
had been round the world, and Ramsay MacDonald had
been in the United States, Canada and South Africa, as
well as making visits to the Continent. Some leading socialists were pacifists—and blindly believed in international
brotherhood and goodwill. But complacency as to the progress of the world was widespread. There had been no
general European war since 1815. The nineteenth century
had brought to western Europe, especially to Britain, a growing prosperity, and in Britain, safeguarded by the sea and
by its sea power, there had grown up a sense of security.
There had, indeed, been a considerable growth in international organisation and ideas. The churches, Roman
Catholic and Protestant, had their international organisations and international conferences. International trade
exhibitions took place, Rotary Clubs were formed, the
Olympic Games were revived. There was a considerable
peace movement, with permanent headquarters in Berne
since 1801, the Nobel peace prizes, the Carnegie endowment
for international peace, the Hague Conferences of 1899 and
1907 on disarmament and arbitration. The economic dependence of the nations on each other was fostered by free
trade and the international growth of capitalism, and was
demonstrated by organisations such as the Universal Postal
Union. The socialists, too, had their international organisations. For Karl Marx the significant division of mankind
was not nationality but class. "Workers of the World,
Unite!" was the international slogan stemming from the
Communist Manifesto of 1848. The first socialist "International" was the International Working Men's Association,
founded in 1864; it was a revolutionary body under the
leadership of Marx and Engels. But it split between the
followers of Marx and those of the Russian anarchist
Bakunin, and faded out in the 1870s. In 1889 the Second
(or Socialist) International was formed—it held a series of
congresses in the pre-war years. A congress was planned to

celebrate the fiftieth anniversary of the First International—
it was planned to meet in Vienna in August 1914. A com-
memorative album was published—prematurely, for the congress never met. Socialist internationalism disappeared with
the rest. At the end of July Keir Hardie was in Brussels to
make preparations for the Vienna Congress. He, Jaurès, the
French socialist leader, and others spoke at a great anti-war
meeting. Two days later Jaurès was assassinated by a French
"patriot", and shortly after the outbreak of war Ramsay
MacDonald described Keir Hardie as "a crushed man" when
he saw him sitting on the terrace of the House of Commons
where Hardie "seemed to be looking out on blank desola-
tion". Hardie was broken by the disappointment and
tragedy of socialists of the different countries slaughtering
each other on the battlefield, and in 1915 he died.

The Labour movement was divided by the war, but did
not split. The ILP opposed it—seeing capitalism and secret
diplomacy as its causes. Ramsay MacDonald (his biographer,
Lord Elton, argues forcefully, that he was not a pacifist)
resigned his chairmanship of the Labour Parliamentary
Party, when the party, forty strong, swung over to support
of the government over the German invasion of Belgium.
Arthur Henderson, a moderate man, became leader. So the
Labour Party supported the Liberal government and the war;
so did the Labour Party Conference at Bristol in 1915. The
ILP did not disaffiliate from the Labour Party in spite of the
divergence of views. The government invited the political parties to co-operate in a recruiting campaign; the Labour Party
agreed, whereas the ILP refused. And in May 1915, when
Asquith formed his coalition government with the Conservatives, he invited the Labour Party also to join, and Arthur
Henderson entered the cabinet (and one or two junior posts
went to Labour)—in spite of scathing ILP comments. The
Labour Party—in a pamphlet of the same year—maintained that its democratic working class aspirations led it to
oppose Germany, for "the victory of Germany would mean

the death of democracy in Europe". Labour membership in the government was strengthened when Lloyd George succeeded Asquith in December 1916. However, there was some unrest in the Glasgow area, and some Labour extremists were imprisoned. The Labour Party treated the ILP with remarkable tolerance, and Ramsay MacDonald, too, strengthened his hold in some ways for the Labour movement recognised the honesty of his opinions and of his action in sacrificing his own position as leader. Labour opponents of the war received less tolerance from the public. Keir Hardie had been all but shouted down in Aberdare; Ramsay Mac-Donald faced hostile crowds in Bradford, London, and Cardiff. The ILP was also in touch, during 1915, with Socialists in foreign countries. Their representatives were refused passports, but an international meeting did take place at Zimmerwald in Switzerland, at which Lenin was present and where the view was pressed that the way to end the war was by revolution against the governments.

Conscription came in 1916, bringing further difficulties over pacificism. Personal resisters to war were organised in the No-Conscription Fellowship; some thousands were imprisoned. Official tribunals were set up to hear the appeals of conscientious objectors, and the *Labour Leader* (the organ of the ILP) supplied in its columns the arguments, religious and otherwise, which objectors should put forward. A leading trade unionist, on the other hand, spoke of conscientious objectors as blacklegs—"Trade unions get rid of blacklegs. I would clear these national blacklegs out of the land". In spite of occasional bitterness, however, the Labour Party held together. The position was anomalous: the Labour Party was a member of the Government, yet its treasurer (Ramsay MacDonald) and four ILP members, together with a handful of Liberals who sided with them over the war, sat on the opposition benches. That even a nominal unity was retained was of immense importance after the war when

the opportunity came to move forward in political importance at the expense of the Liberal Party.

Like the war itself, the Russian Revolution of 1917 was a
challenge to the Labour Party, though at first the full nature
of the challenge was not apparent. The events of the Revolution were but dimly understood. Many months, or years,
would elapse before it became clear that Russia would apply
a socialist policy, but apply it by means of a tyranny un-
acceptable to a Western socialist party which was also
democratic. At first the dilemma did not appear. Of all the
Great Powers, Russia was the most backward, and for long
enough the rule of the tsars had been hated by liberals
and socialists in the West. The first revolution in March
1917, therefore, was welcomed, and a group calling itself
the United Socialist Council (actually responsible were the
ILP together with the British Socialist Party—a forerunner
of the Communist Party) arranged a meeting in Leeds to
express solidarity with the workmen and soldiers of Russia.
The meeting, which took place in June and was attended
by twelve hundred delegates, showed a certain revolutionary
fervour. There were now moves for contacts with Russia and
a possible end to the war by negotiation. Arthur Henderson
was sent by Lloyd George on a visit to Russia. British Labour
representatives were invited to visit Petrograd; but when
they reached Aberdeen the seamen refused to take them.
Proposals were made for a socialist conference in Stockholm,
but the Allied Governments, fearing the effect on the war
effort of such a conference, refused passports. Arthur Henderson, who had supported the Stockholm proposal, resigned,
but his place was filled by George Barnes and Labour continued in the Government. In November, came the second
Russian revolution, the economic revolution, when Lenin
and the communists seized power. This time the Labour
attitude was more guarded; some like Philip Snowden were
critical, because the revolution had not come by parliamentary means, others like Fred Jowett welcomed "the sweeping

away of the entire capitalist system" although, later on, he did admit that "the excesses in the revolution were distasteful".

Victory in war was followed immediately by a victory election in December 1918. It was the first general election since 1910, for parliament had prolonged its own life during the war. Lloyd George fought the election as Coalition leader; he had the full backing of the Conservative Party, its leader, Bonar Law, being one of his closest colleagues, and of a large part of the Liberal Party. Coalition candidates received what Asquith scornfully called the "coupon", a letter of personal endorsement signed by Lloyd George and Bonar Law. Opposed to the Coalition was the independent Liberal Party under Asquith and the Labour Party (although a handful of Labour MPs stayed with the Coalition and received the coupon). The election was fought in an atmosphere of excitement and emotion. Lloyd George, "the man who won the war", proposed to make Germany pay the whole cost of the war and spoke of making Britain a "fit country for heroes to live in". The victory of the Coalition was overwhelming; it won 474 seats, of which 338 were Conservative and 136 Liberal. The independent Liberals were reduced to 26, and Asquith himself was defeated. In effect, Lloyd George had widened and perpetuated the split among the Liberals, and all but destroyed the Liberal Party. The Labour Party lost its leading figures—Arthur Henderson was defeated as well as the anti-war leaders, Ramsay MacDonald and Snowden—but increased its members from 42 to 59 and became the Opposition.

For the moment Lloyd George's victory was complete. During the election, he had stigmatised Labour as "being run by the extreme pacifist, Bolshevist Group", and for the present he dominated the political scene. But when in 1922 the Conservatives became anxious for the independence of their party and decided at their Carlton Club meeting to leave the Coalition, Lloyd George resigned, and never came back to power. What was significant about the 1918 election was, in the long run, the disintegration of the Liberal Party and its replacement by the Labour Party. In spite of winning the war, the fact that Lloyd George had pushed out Asquith was never forgiven; personal rancour and rivalry divided the two factions in the Liberal Party; the existence of two leaders, of two ex-premiers, made unity impossible. When, in the general election of 1922, the three parties fought separately, the results were : Conservative 347, Labour 142, Liberal 118, divided into two groups, one following Asquith, the other Lloyd George. Henceforth the Liberals remained weaker than Labour, and the Labour Party took its place as second party in the traditional two-party system. And leading Labour figures, defeated in 1918, now came back to parliament : Ramsay MacDonald, Snowden, Jowett. J. R. Clynes and J. H. Thomas retained their seats, and Arthur Henderson returned after a by-election early in 1923. Mac-Donald was elected leader, replacing Clynes.

Behind the political struggle in the successive post-war elections lay the underlying fact that the Labour Party stood for a socialist policy (which broadly appealed to the working classes). Whereas the Liberal Party supported the system of private enterprise. The Conservative Party even more strongly was a capitalist party. Why, then, have two such parties? The weaker of the two, the Liberal Party, inevitably declined.

The Labour Party in 1918 had moved definitely to a socialist policy. Arthur Henderson, whose honesty and integrity made their mark in the closing months of the war, gave special attention (calling in the help of Sidney Webb) to the re-organisation of the party and the making of a programme. The new constitution of the Labour Party, adopted in February 1918, turned the party from a loose federation of affiliated organisations (the trade unions and the various socialist societies) into a centralised party with party discipline but with individual members belonging to their local branch in each constituency. The trade unions, though, were predominant, both financially and in weight of numbers. The famous Clause 4—echoing the ILP resolution of a quarter of a century earlier—stated the socialist aim of the party: "to secure for the workers by hand or by brain the full fruits of their industry and the most equitable distribution thereof that may be possible, upon the basis of the common ownership of the means of production". (The words "distribution and exchange" were added at the party conference in 1929). At a party conference in June the new programme, *Labour and the New Social Order,* was adopted. It put forward the socialist policy—though still avoiding the use of the word socialism. "We need," the manifesto declared, "to beware of patchwork. The view of the Labour Party is that what has to be reconstructed after the war is not this or that government department, or this or that piece of social machinery; but, so far as Britain is concerned, society itself."

With the adoption of the socialist aim for the Labour Party the trade unions had moved further than ever before, to the left. This is to be explained, at least in part, by their experience of wartime government controls. There had indeed been a notable exercise of government control for the public good in wartime. Why not, then, for the public good in peacetime also? As J. H. Thomas, speaking at the June conference, put it : "The taking over of railways, mines and munitions factories and other controlled establishments during the war really meant that in the considered judgment of the Government . . . the private ownership of these things in time of war was a danger to the State". Ordinary trade unionists had experienced government control in wartime and had found in it various advantages, regular wages, secure employment, indeed, one might say, full employment.

The nation had won victory in the war, Lloyd George victory in the 1918 General Election, yet at the same time the Labour Party found a new confidence and the trade unionists, indeed, the whole working class, a new determina-

tion. All wished to gain some tangible result from the prolonged sufferings of the world war. The following years,
therefore, were disturbed ones. There was resentment at slow
demobilisation, and the year 1919 opened with fears of a
general strike—and the fear of revolution was not far away
with the example of Russia in people's minds. In Glasgow
there was serious trouble in January and February; the
factories were closed, the red flag was hoisted, and troops
had to be called up to march through the streets. Strikes
and threats of strikes—pressing for better conditions and
higher wages—continued throughout 1919, 1920, and 1921.
There was a police strike in 1919, a nationwide railway
strike later in the same year, and a miners' strike in 1920 and
in 1921—the latter almost leading to a general strike, under
the leadership of the Triple Industrial Alliance of Miners, Railwaymen, and Transport Workers formed in 1914. But it
was averted when the leaders of the railwaymen and transport workers decided against extreme action on what came
to be known by the miners as "Black Friday" (April 15th,
1921). The miners had pressed hard for nationalisation of
the mines, and there was a good deal of sympathy for their
cause. Lloyd George had appointed the Sankey Commission
(under Lord Sankey, later to be Lord Chancellor in the
Labour Government), in 1919, but it did not produce a
unanimous report and this enabled the Government to avoid
taking action.

The year 1920 saw the beginnings of a separate Communist Party formed out of various Marxist groups, such as
the British Socialist Party. This move was inspired by the
founding of the Third International by the Bolsheviks in
the previous year. The new Communist Party, following a
tactic of infiltration, applied for affiliation to the Labour
Party, but was refused—the first refusal of many.

The Labour Party's opportunity came at the end of 1923.
Bonar Law had formed a Conservative Government on the
break-up of the Coalition and the resignation of Lloyd

George, but Bonar Law himself had to give up because of ill-health in May 1923. Stanley Baldwin followed as Conservative premier. He had made his reputation as a man of commonsense and goodwill. He had feared that the result of Lloyd George's leadership of the Coalition might be to destroy the independence of the Conservative Party, but his own first moves resulted in losing it an election. For Baldwin thought he must turn to protective duties to deal with unemployment, and decided to go to the country to secure a mandate for the new policy. The attack on the traditional free trade policy of the Liberals united Asquith and Lloyd George, at least temporarily, and the Liberal Party recovered some ground. Labour had 191 members, and the Liberals 158; together they outnumbered the Conservatives. What was to happen now? No one had expected such a situation : some regarded Labour as bent on the destruction of the whole social order, others, who perhaps knew better, thought they must be given their chance—in all events they would be in a minority in parliament, and, if they could not govern, they would soon discredit themselves. Thus when Baldwin met parliament in January 1924 the Liberals voted with Labour to turn out the Conservatives, and the king called upon Ramsay MacDonald to form a government. There was, as in the days of Keir Hardie, some popular excitement about dress. Morning dress and top hats were required when the ministers saw the king—most of the Labour ministers wore it, but Jowett and Wheatley appeared in their ordinary suits, and a soft hat and bowler respectively. However, the king was satisfied; he recorded in his diary : "they all seem to be very intelligent and they take things very seriously". J. R. Clynes wrote later on : "As we stood waiting for His Majesty, amid the gold and crimson of the Palace, I could not help marvelling at the strange turn of Fortune's wheel, which had brought MacDonald the starveling clerk, Thomas the engine-driver, Henderson the foundry labourer and Clynes the mill-hand, to this pinnacle beside the man whose forebears had been kings for so many generations. We were making history".

They were, indeed, making history. But Labour was in office not in power; they depended on Liberal votes. And, in any case, no socialist legislation was forthcoming. At a meeting of leaders before taking office (MacDonald, Snowden, Sidney Webb, J. H. Thomas and Henderson) two possible courses had been examined : to introduce a socialist programme and be defeated, or to put forward only measures which it would be possible to carry. The latter course was adopted. Even so before the end of the year Labour was defeated over its proposal to make a trade agreement with Bolshevik Russia. During the election in October there appeared in the press the Zinoviev letter[1]—purporting to give Communist instructions for subversion in the armed forces—and with the help of *Daily Mail* headlines, "Moscow Orders to Our Reds—Great Plot Disclosed", a strong Conservative reaction followed giving Baldwin a secure majority with 415 members in the House.

The 1924 election result, though a great victory for the Conservatives, was not in other respects a disaster for Labour. Fear of the Reds had led to a swing to the right— from the Liberals rather than from Labour. The Liberal Party was all but destroyed and never recovered. Many Liberals (their poll fell by $1\frac{1}{4}$ million) voted Conservative as did many people who had not troubled to vote in 1923. Although they lost 40 seats, the Labour vote increased by over a million (from 4,348,379 to 5,482,620). Nor was Labour discredited—its supporters had the excuse that the Labour government had been tied by its dependence on Liberal support.

The first Labour Government marked the highwater of the tide of opportunity which flowed from the war. During

[1] The letter was almost certainly a forgery made by White Russian refugees in Berlin in order to discredit the Anglo-Soviet trade negotiations. See L. Chester (and others): *The Zinoviev Letter* (1969).

the war the workers had begun to feel their strength. Not only had the trade union leaders had to be treated with a new respect, but rank and file movements on the shop floor led by shop stewards showed considerable activity. Lloyd George had had to use great circumspection in dealing with the organised workers; strikes, which interfered with the war effort might be declared illegal, but the government could not in fact put thousands of striking workers in prison. After the war the miners were in the van with their demand for nationalisation, the TUC and Labour Party launched a joint campaign with the slogan "The Mines for the Nation", and co-operated in other ways also. The years since 1914 had seen a remarkable growth in trade union strength, from four millions in 1914 to eight millions in 1920, though there was a big fall in the next two years, and also a strengthening of the TUC with, since 1921, the building up of the administrative machinery of its General Council. Much of the strength of the Labour Party sprang from the unions.

Yet in spite of the close connection between the unions and the Labour Party, the Labour government of 1924 when faced with strikes had to make arrangements very similar to those of other governments; for example, to meet a strike of dockers the government had arranged to use troops to move essential supplies. The union leaders quickly realised that, in the words of a speaker at the 1925 TUC, "even with a complete Labour majority in the House, and with a Labour Government . . . there would be a permanent difference in point of view between the government on the one hand and the trade unions on the other". The failure of the first Labour government and disillusion with political activity turned the unions back to industrial action, and so led on to the General Strike.

The continuing strength—and, some would say, weakness —of the Labour movement was demonstrated by the General Strike in 1926. Economic depression and consequent industrial unrest had continued, and came to a head over the miners' wages. The coal owners, in order to sell in foreign markets, tried to lower prices by reducing wages. The miners refused, and won general support among the unions. The miners put their case to the General Council of the Trades Union Congress. There was deadlock with the coal owners. But the government bought time by giving a subsidy for miners' wages on Red Friday (July 31st, 1925, and setting up a royal commission. When the subsidy came to an end on April 30th, 1926, miners and owners were still deadlocked. And this time there was no "Black Friday". The General Council of the Trades Union Congress organised the General Strike for May 3rd. Factories stopped, transport halted, newspapers failed to appear. Action on such a scale appeared not merely a strike, but a blow at the country as a whole. The Government took counter-action to provide essential supplies and services. Both sides faced the prospect of revolution. But moderate councils prevailed : the strike leaders were not willing for revolution. Behind the scenes negotiations were opened, and the TUC called off the strike on May 12th (though the miners continued, and had in the end to accept wage reductions). The General Strike was a most remarkable episode : it made clear to both sides how far they could go. And that it passed off without revolution showed how little real bitterness there was between class and class, or, to put it another way, how great was the underlying social cohesion in the country.

The next opportunity for Labour came in 1929. Prolonged unemployment was the most marked feature of the time, and the Liberals—led by Lloyd George and backed by the economist Keynes—put forward a bold plan of public works. But they failed to win the necessary support. The Labour Party won the election, and with 287 seats was for the first time the largest party; a second Labour government took office under Ramsay MacDonald, though once more dependent on Liberal votes in parliament. But the second Labour government was unlucky : it was caught in the world slump, the worst slump in history, which had started with the Wall Street crash of October. World trade collapsed catastrophically, and unemployment mounted—at its worst, there were three million unemployed in Britain, six million in Germany, and twelve million in the U.S.A. By the middle of 1931 there was serious financial difficulty in Britain. The Labour government was unable to deal with the growing unemployment, and the May Committee reported that the cost of relief was unbalancing the budget. Drastic cuts were necessary to avoid bankruptcy. This led to a financial crisis: foreigners withdrew deposits from the Bank of England, and the Bank had to ask France and America for aid. The government prepared to make cuts—consultations were held with Liberal and Conservative leaders—but could not get agreement inside the government to make a ten per cent cut in the dole. MacDonald was in close touch with the other political leaders (but not with Lloyd George, who was seriously ill at the time) and the king. He was persuaded to bring his Labour government to an end and to head a new government. In August MacDonald resigned as prime minister of the Labour government, and was thereupon called on by the king to form a new National Government, consisting of his own personal Labour supporters, Conservatives, and Liberals. His action marked a bitter break in the Labour Party; there was a feeling that MacDonald had betrayed them, and in the following month he was expelled. Cuts were made in expenditure, and in October a general election took place. The Conservatives came back with 471 seats; the Labour Party had 52. Its vote dropped by nearly two millions. It was an overwhelming defeat for Labour— socialism was indefinitely postponed.

9. Socialism: Theory and Practice

THERE HAD BEEN two socialist governments—but no socialism. What had happened? There was a glaring difference between socialist theory and practice, though no one wished to draw attention to the subject. At least, not publicly. But Beatrice Webb, in February 1931, wrote boldly enough in her diary : "Ramsay MacDonald and Snowden and many other Labour Front Bench men, in their heart of hearts, do not wish a *change in policy*. It is an absurdity that the Labour Party, as at present constituted, should be in power. The Labour Movement had better be referred to its studies ... it has completely lost its bearings". The socialists themselves (apart from left wing critics of their leaders) were naturally unwilling to recognise their failure to produce socialism, whereas Conservatives and Liberals were relieved that nothing untoward had happened and hoped that the subject could be forgotten. Labour supporters when tackled about the failure of the Labour governments fell back on the argument that they had been in office but not in power, and had depended for their existence on the Liberal members in parliament. In a sense the argument was fair enough, but much less so in 1929 when the Liberals had ready a much bolder policy for dealing with unemployment than the Labour ministers ever produced. Labour supporters, perhaps, were coming to expect less of socialism than they had once expected—though in their meetings and publications they went on repeating the old slogans. After all, few, if any, human movements have achieved their objectives completely or to the satisfaction of all. The struggle for the vote—but who can confidently say today that democratic government solves all political problems? Free trade—once it was an economic and political doctrine that ranged party against party, but now is almost forgotten. Was its importance exaggerated? Party itself—if any one party were ever completely successful in achieving its aims and satisfying the people, would not other parties and further elections be unnecessary? Old aims—achieved in part or unachieved, are replaced by new. Was the same kind of thing happening to socialism?

Perhaps, to some extent, it was. But whatever happened to socialism, the Labour Party was not finished, in spite of its great defeat in 1931 and the difficulties which followed. At the next election, in 1935—the last until the end of the Second World War—the Labour Party recovered much of its lost ground. It was now led by Clement Attlee, who succeeded George Lansbury. With a poll of 8,326,000 votes (as against 6,648,000 in 1931 and 8,380,000 in 1929) it won 154 seats. The Liberals were but a handful, and divided into hostile groups. The Labour Party was the Opposition, was the only possible alternative to the Conservatives at some future date. The Labour Party—whatever its theory, whether socialist or not—represented a solid working class strength in the country and could not be ignored. It might need a new policy, or it might need a modification of the old policy, but in a two-party system of government the Labour Party with its eight million votes was the other one of the two parties.

There were a number of other reasons why the virtual disappearance of socialism from the political arena came about so easily and did not arouse more attention. Whatever party was in office, the ordinary, day-to-day work of government had to go on. This the Labour governments—in spite of their inexperience—had managed to do. Ramsay MacDonald had every intention of showing that Labour was fit to govern and of allaying fears that he and his ministers were a wild, irresponsible lot. The Labour leaders were on the whole cautious men. They were not young, and they had achieved remarkable success in getting to the top of the political ladder. They did not wish to endanger their comparative prosperity by taking risks. And as they had grown older, and more prosperous, they had doubtless become more conservative as so often happens. Many Labour men, too, on entering the House of Commons were genuinely astonished at what they found—and impressed, as was Clynes by the king and the gold and crimson of the palace. In spite of occasional scenes in the House, even the wild men of the Labour Party came under the subtle, restraining influence of the establishment. MacDonald, of course, through his wife and his own personal inclinations, had contacts with the great and influential, but many of the Labour men were surprised to find that "the Great Ones, the Powerful Ones, the Lordly Ones", as David Kirkwood from Clydeside described them, whom they had pictured ruthlessly suppressing the working class, were in fact unaffected and friendly and even sympathetic to the claims of working people. In and out of parliament the Labour members of parliament came in for a lot of attention which was flattering and pleasing. When James Maxton, another Clydesider, visited the Oxford Union he was lionised by the undergraduates.

The width and vagueness of Labour theory and policy was also a weakness. The reconstruction of "society itself", as put forward in *Labour and the New Social Order*, was an all embracing aim which could mean everything or nothing. Socialism itself was open to different interpretations by different people, state socialism or guild socialism, for example, to go no further. And how to put into force any such policy was altogether different from expressing it in general terms on the political platform; to attack private property was one thing, to confiscate the possessions of their friends on the opposite side of the House was quite another. At this point, therefore, it is worthwhile to look at the development in socialist thinking which had been going on since the *Fabian Essays* of 1889.

The Labour Party attached special importance to its principles. As *Labour and the New Social Order* put it in 1918, "whatever may be the case with regard to other political parties, our detailed practical proposals proceed from definitely held principles". And it was the view of the Labour Party that "society itself" had to be reconstructed. It regarded the war as dealing a death-blow to "the individualist system of capitalist production, based on the private ownership and competitive administration of land and capital . . . we shall do our utmost to see that it is buried with the millions whom it has done to death". Then came an outline of Labour's policy. "The Four Pillars of the House that we propose to erect . . . may be termed :

(a) The Universal Enforcement of the National Minimum;
(b) The Democratic Control of Industry;
(c) The Revolution in National Finance; and
(d) The Surplus Wealth for the Common Good."

Under the first head, "the first principle of the Labour Party —in significant contrast with those of the Capitalist System, whether expressed by the Liberal or by the Conservative Party—is the securing to every member of the community . . . of all the requisites of healthy life and worthy citizenship". This meant the setting of national minimum standards below which none should fall, the prevention of unemployment— by the government taking measures to "arrange the public works and the orders of National Departments and Local Authorities in such a way as to maintain the aggregate demand for labour in the whole kingdom (including that of capitalist employers) approximately at a uniform level from year to year", and, if such measures should fail, the provision of adequate maintenance. The revolution in national finance meant not only changes in the use of direct taxation—income tax and super-tax—but also a great increase in death duties and an out-and-out "conscription of wealth" or Capital levy, steeply graduated, to pay off a substantial part of the national debt. The surplus for the common good indicated that Labour would transfer that surplus—"the extra profits of the fortunate capitalists . . . devoted very largely to the senseless luxury of an idle rich class"—to public use. "It is from this constantly arising Surplus (to be secured, on the one hand, by Nationalisation and Municipalisation and, on the other, by the steeply graduated Taxation of Private Income and Riches) that will have to be found the new capital which the community day by day needs for the perpetual improvement and increase of its various enterprises, for which we shall decline to be dependent on the usury-exacting financiers. . . ."

It was under the second heading that the manifesto asserted its distinctive socialist principle—"the Labour Party insists on Democracy in industry as well as in government. It demands the progressive elimination from the control of industry of the private capitalist. . . . What the Labour Party looks to is a genuinely scientific reorganisation of the nation's industry, no longer deflected by individual profiteering, on the basis of the Common Ownership of the Means of Production". This meant the nationalisation of land, railways, mines, electric power, and health insurance; the extension of local government to cover services such as the supply of coal and milk; and the maintenance of wartime government controls over imports, shipping, and food and clothing industries.

In the 1920 edition of *Fabian Essays*, Sidney Webb considered how far there had been changes in socialist thinking since the first edition had appeared in 1889. The economics, the basis of socialism, he thought to be sound. But fault could be found with the historical treatment. The early Fabians had not realised the importance of the trade union movement; similarly they were not at first appreciative of the co-operative movement although the Webbs themselves remedied this situation by their massive publications on these subjects during the 1890s. Nor had they fully realised the importance which municipal socialism would take on, both as giving practical experience of collectivism and "in the placing, by 1919, of literally thousands of members of the Labour Party on local governing bodies". And although they held to nationalisation in principle, they were vague as to practical proposals. Here was a difficulty which the two Labour Governments were to find in practice. To state the theoretical antithesis between private ownership for private profit, and public ownership for the public good was not difficult. To see the replacement of the private by the public system in practical terms was difficult.

Just as the international socialist movement was, and is, split between those who believe in socialism by revolution and those who see it coming by democratic means, so has British socialism been divided between those who really believed in a complete replacement of the capitalist system by a socialist system and those others (many of whom had been or might well have been Liberals if the Liberal Party had maintained its strength) who looked for slow, gradual change or even only for piecemeal social reform. And however moderate the Labour governments proved in practice, the Labour Party was in its principles and theory committed to a utopian policy of social revolution. The Labour Party, indeed, saw itself as more than a party, as part of the socialist movement. This had its own mystique, its own half-conscious millenary expectations going back to Robert Owen and beyond, back to Christendom—the new view of society, the new social order, the new economic system of socialism. Thus there was an inherent conflict between the soul of the movement, its inmost traditions and aspirations, its theoretical principles, and what the movement actually achieved when the Labour governments took office—just as there is all too often a conflict between the teachings of Christ which inspired the church and the every day actions and behaviour of ordinary Christians.

It was this belief in a change of system that characterised the Labour Party in the period between the wars. As many of us recall, and as Professor Samuel H. Beer of Harvard has pointed out, "such system-thinking informed the standard rhetoric of the party at conferences and in parliament, in socialist tracts, routine propaganda, and comprehensive statements of purpose". The policy statement of 1918 had warned against patchwork and aimed at the reconstruction of "society itself". Later policy statements followed the same line. In 1928 Ramsay MacDonald prefaced *Labour and the Nation* with : "The Labour Party, unlike other parties, is not concerned with patching the rents in a bad system, but with transforming Capitalism into Socialism." The programme expressed its aim : "To secure for the producers by hand or by brain the full fruits of their industry, and the most equitable distribution thereof that may be possible, upon the basis of the common ownership of the means of production. . . . The Labour Party is a Socialist party." A few years later in 1934, *For Socialism and Peace* explained that the nation had to choose between patching up capitalism and a socialist reconstruction of the national life. "There is no halfway house," the manifesto stated, "between a society based on private ownership of the means of production with the profit of the few as the measure of success, and a society where public ownership of those means enables the resources of the nation to be deliberately planned for attaining the maximum of general well being." The statement expressed the aim : "to convert industry . . . from a haphazard struggle for private gain to a planned national economy owned by and carried on for the service of the community". Other Labour pamphlets expressed the same theme : "capitalism is dying . . . socialism is the only alternative". In 1937 the new leader of the party, Major Clement Attlee, speaking of the evils of capitalism, said : "The cause is private property; the remedy is public ownership".

Yet at the very same time that the Labour Party was committed to a fundamental change of the social system the other, and at least to some extent opposed, point of view was gaining strength. Indeed Sidney Webb's contribution to the original *Fabian Essays* had pointed out the extent to which socialism—through government and municipal controls and social services—had already developed in Britain. And when Bernard Shaw contributed a preface to the edition of 1931 (as Webb had done in 1920) he rejoiced in the longevity of the *Essays* and their continuing influence. There had indeed been a large degree of socialist permeation in social development and in people's thinking—"Everything that is contained in the essays should by this time have become part of the common education of every citizen".

Ramsay MacDonald wrote several books about socialism before the war, but his *Socialism: Critical and Constructive* which appeared in 1921 can be taken as summing up his mature and considered thinking. The title itself indicates a socialism which can be critical of abuses but is to be constructive, not revolutionary. He saw "the emergence of socialism"—not its revolutionary establishment. "Progress," he says, in accord with his youthful interests in natural science and biological evolution, "consists in the adaptation of man in his circumstances. . . . Capitalism has marked a stage in the evolution of social organisation on its material side . . . it has brought material efficiency to a high stage of perfection." But now it has become too big to be left to boards of directors —"Society itself is steadily stepping in and is gaining authority over itself by controlling the material powers and organisation of capitalism".

Indeed MacDonald's book was remarkably persuasive in argument and tone. Occasionally he might appear to lash out. He showed, historically, how land had become private: by conquest, by confiscation (e.g. the dissolution of the monasteries and the seizure of their lands), by enclosures—"by great and simple acts of wholesale theft". But he does not overlook what has happened since. "Since then, of course, the lands thus confiscated have been bought and sold, mortgaged . . . and have become inextricably woven into our fabric of private possession." The government must approach the problem warily, and tackle it gradually. In general, "to talk of abolishing property is folly" and he defends property which is the reward of services. In short, MacDonald stresses the idea of reasoned progress, evolution, transition, and he concludes on the note—"Socialism a Fulfilment". But what socialism meant to different socialists was not necessarily the same. Conflicting views appeared at the party conference in 1927 to discuss the new policy statement published the following year as *Labour and the Nation*. Bevin spoke for a programme not over the heads of the people, for many trade unionists were not socialists; Cook and Maxton urged a full-blooded socialism, while Ramsay MacDonald made an eloquent speech on socialism which, according to Cole, turned out "to mean absolutely nothing".

In 1937, when the Labour Party had struggled back to influence after the debacle of 1931, a new voice spoke out with the old message—or was it? Douglas Jay, with a brilliant academic career in classics at Winchester and New College, an economic and financial journalist destined for high office in future Labour governments, published *The Socialist Case*. If it was indeed the case for socialism, it was the case for a different kind of socialism; or at least it was the case for a policy which put much less emphasis on the older belief in public ownership and the change of system and much more emphasis on financial controls (through taxation) which could reduce the poverty and unemployment within the capitalist system. "The purpose of this book," Mr Jay stated, "is to sum up the case for socialism on the basis of an examination of the fact of poverty. . . . It is written in the belief that the fundamental case for socialism rests on the necessity to alleviate economic privation." Next he says that the book "seeks to sum up the case for socialism in the light of the practical experience and the scientific advances gained in the years of the Great Depression and the succeeding armaments boom," and he goes on to express his great indebtedness to the writings of J. M. Keynes. This suggests a shift of emphasis—the use of financial measures, through taxation and the expansion of credit, instead of replacing the capitalist system by a socialist system, especially as he says at the end of the book, that "there is no economic reason why a modern industrial State, under the kind of leadership which the Social-Democrats have given Sweden, M. Blum has given France, and Mr Roosevelt has given the United States in the last five years, should not simultaneously overcome the forces of the trade cycle and redistribute the incomes of the rich". He might also have mentioned the Lloyd George policy, *We can conquer Unemployment*, backed by the economic thinking of Keynes, which must have influenced him as early as 1929—and, even Hitler, whose rearmament policy worked an economic miracle in the National Socialist Germany of 1933-39.

But this was not the socialism, hitherto, of the Labour Party; this was not the socialism of a thousand passionate meetings in which a change of system had been promised. Public ownership was to replace private capitalism. But about public ownership and nationalisation (only some six pages in a long book) Mr Jay was very guarded. "Socialists have been mistaken," he wrote, "in making ownership of the means of production instead of ownership of inherited property the test of socialisation. . . . It is not the ownership of the means of production as such, but ownership of large inherited incomes, which ought to be eliminated."[1] Discussing the problem of redistributing incomes in a modern industrial state, he maintains that "it must not be supposed that nationalisation or 'socialisation' is in itself any solution to the problem".

Unless the state confiscated out-and-out, the private shareholder will receive state bonds in return for his shares, and there will not be any redistribution of income. To do this, the method is taxation, and modification of inheritance laws. Later, Mr Jay asks: "What should we nationalise?", and the very question must have shaken the older kind of socialist. Large-scale undertakings which are, or have become, monopolies may rightly be nationalised; the advantages of com-

---

[1] Certain other socialist writers had already been moving in this direction, e.g. Hugh Dalton in *Inequalities of Incomes in Modern Communities* (1920) suggesting increased use of death duties, and R. H. Tawney in *The Acquisitive Society* (1921) and *Equality* (1931). Neither put great stress on nationalisation.

petition have disappeared, there are economies in large scale operation, and a private monopoly can exploit the consumer. Such undertakings were the railways, the mines, road transport, banking, electricity, gas, iron and steel, and a number of other industries. But "it must be admitted that there is a very large class of industries to which nationalisation would only be appropriate at a very late stage, if ever," such industries including the very small, the speculative, and new trades. And "one of the most real of all the dangers of socialism . . . is the danger of discouraging the undertaking of speculative risks . . . for many of the greatest industries grow out of such beginnings". In addition, there is an important class of industries, where the industry is not a monopoly and is not small and speculative—over these some form of public control might be exercised.

In his final chapter, called like his book "The Case for Socialism", he asserted that "the case for socialism is mainly economic, and it rests on fact". The greatest economists have, in fact, recognised the weaknesses in the capitalist system to which socialists have drawn attention—the arbitrary effects of so-called free exchange (as, for example, when a rich man exchanges with a poor man), the unfair character of unearned incomes, and the anti-social consequences of inheritance—and he quoted the economists from Mill and Marshall to Pigou and Keynes to demonstrate the point. Then he came to what was, for him, the application of socialism—"the drastic application of a socialist policy does not necessarily involve, for economic reasons, a revolutionary break with the methods of social reform that have been followed in the last century in democratic countries. The progressive expansion of the social services, the steady expansion of social ownership and control, and the even more drastic modification of property and inheritance rights—all these are policies which need not cause any violent upheaval in the machinery of the economic system." So he saw the prospect of peaceful development—without the appeal to revolution or without revolution provoking war. "There is no economic reason," he declared, "why a clash of this kind must be inevitable." It would seem, therefore, that socialism in the hands of Mr Jay had taken a big step away from "system-thinking" and towards a progressive policy of social reform and financial controls which might be as acceptable to Liberals as to socialists. He had, in a sense, stated a policy for achieving the objectives of socialism, without socialism. Mr Jay was a precursor of things to come, and in his preface he stated that Hugh Gaitskell had read the typescript—Gaitskell the future leader of the Labour Party, who many years later attempted to amend the famous Clause IV of the party constitution—"the common ownership of the means of production, distribution and exchange".[1]

10. The General Strike

APART FROM THE two Labour governments, there were two episodes of the inter-war years which for the whole British socialist movement were traumatic experiences—the general strike and the development of Soviet Russia. Labour electoral victories and the two Labour governments indicated the great numerical strength of the Labour movement, but at the same time the growth in numbers marked a dilution of the early fervour and a discrepancy between theory and practice. In the same way the general strike was witness to the strength and discipline of the industrial forces of Labour, but it proved a high point beyond which industrial action could not go. Soviet Russia, too, might win praise and

[1] Gaitskell, in a lecture published in 1956—*Recent Developments in British Socialist thinking*—paid a high tribute to Douglas Jay's book and his clear realisation of the significance of Keynes for Socialist thought.

admiration in theory, and at a safe distance, but basically British socialists sensed that Russian conditions were not British conditions, and what might be appropriate in Russia could never be right in Britain. And here lay the dilemma of the strikers: the use of massed industrial power to gain economic objectives seemed, on the one hand, a natural development of the Labour movement, but on the other it posed the question, if the government resisted, of whether the strikers were ready and willing to go on to a revolutionary take-over of the government.

The idea of a general strike was not new. Various alliances of the bigger unions had considered it: the Triple Alliance had been in 1921 on the brink of a general stoppage, and again in 1925 the government had faced concerted pressure by the big unions and had put off the evil day by temporary surrender in giving a subsidy in support of the miners' wages. After the strike itself was over a young American professor visited this country and made a study of the events, publishing in 1931 a lengthy book entitled: *The General Strike: A Study of Labor's Tragic Weapon in Theory and Practice*. In the early days, in 1832, a socialistic agitator, William Benbow, had published a pamphlet, *The Grand National Holiday, and Congress of the Productive Classes*, advocating a stoppage of work for one month which would bring to a standstill both production and government. Then, in their Congress, the workers would make new laws—"Equal rights, equal liberties, equal enjoyments, equal toil, equal respect, equal share of production: this is the object of our holy day," he wrote. Some attempt at action by means of a general strike was planned by the leaders of the Grand National Consolidated Trades Union in 1833-4 under the aegis of Robert Owen. John Doherty held such ideas. The Chartists talked of a national holiday or sacred month. Georges Sorel (1847-1922), the French syndicalist, saw the importance of some great irrational myth as an impulse to proletarian action, and the idea of the general strike could be such a myth. But his ideas were more influential among the fascists in Italy and Germany than among British trade unionists. The trade union leader, Tom Mann, writing in 1911 regarded the general strike as a revolutionary weapon. "We shall always do our best," he wrote, "to help strikers to be successful and we shall prepare the way as rapidly as possible for the General Strike of national proportions. The workers will refuse any longer to manipulate the machinery of production in the interests of the capitalist class and there will be no power on earth to compel them to work when they thus refuse." It was not difficult, therefore, for the more extreme union leaders to see the general strike as an event which would bring down the government. But within the Labour movement there were profound differences of view—even among trade unionists. A. J. Cook of the miners and J. H. Thomas of the railwaymen represented strongly opposed positions, neatly crystallised in a theatrical revue put on by the Liberal Summer School:

> Cook : "I am the miners' king,
>   The General Strike's the thing."
> Thomas : "I am the railway tsar,
>   The General Strike I bar."

Indeed there was a strong antipathy between Cook and Thomas. Thomas, on one occasion, described Cook as a b—— swine.

Thus, when the strike started on May 3rd, though there was a remarkably united response by the rank-and-file, there was much heart-searching and anxiety among the leaders. The TUC was careful to disclaim any political objective, and to maintain that the strike was industrial in character. In the first issue of the *British Worker*, a paper produced under the auspices of the TUC, there was on the front page a "Message to All Workers":

"The General Council of the Trades Union Congress

wishes to emphasise the fact that this is an industrial dispute. It expects every member taking part to be exemplary in his conduct and not to give any opportunities for police interference. The outbreak of any disturbances would be very damaging to the prospects of a successful termination of the dispute."

Throughout the strike the General Council was anxious and careful to maintain control over the strikers in all parts of the country, and to answer allegations that they were a disorderly lot. The respectability of the strikers was asserted; they were not to be portrayed or regarded as revolutionaries.

The parliamentary Labour leaders instinctively feared the strike—it might take control out of their hands and give it to industrial forces outside parliament. Ramsay MacDonald and Snowden both saw the strike as a threat to the gradual, peaceful, parliamentary way of changing society. J. H. Thomas had a similar fear. "What I dreaded about this strike more than anything else was this," he said later, "that it should pass into revolutionary hands. If by any chance it should have got out of the hands of those who would be able to exercise some control, every sane man knows what would have happened. . . . That danger, that fear, was always in our minds, because we wanted at least even in this struggle to direct a disciplined army." And too many questions had been left open : what were the precise aims of the strike? how long should it go on? how were people to be fed during the strike?

The more general view—and what might be termed the official view—was that the general strike was a threat to the country. The prime minister, Stanley Baldwin, speaking on May 3rd in the House of Commons, portrayed the issue as a challenge to constitutional government—though his speech was conciliatory in tone. Stronger in tone was the editor of the *Daily Mail*, in an editorial which the printers refused to print—an incident which helped to precipitate the strike :

"A general strike is not an industrial dispute. It is a revolutionary movement intended to inflict suffering upon the

great mass of innocent persons in the community and thereby
to put forcible constraint upon the Government.

"It is a movement which can only succeed by destroying
the Government and subverting the rights and liberties of
the people.

"This being the case, it cannot be tolerated by any civilised
Government and it must be dealt with by every resource at
the disposal of the community. . . .

"We call upon all law-abiding men and women to hold
themselves at the service of King and Country."

In the House of Commons, a leading Liberal, Sir John
Simon, who had been home secretary under Asquith and had
a great reputation as a lawyer, condemned the strike in measured, legal terms: "A strike, properly understood, is per-
fectly legal . . . (but) the decision of the Council of the Trade
Union Executives, to call out everybody, regardless of the
contracts which these workmen had made, was not a lawful
act at all." Thus all workers who were bound by contract
had, Simon argued, broken the law, and were liable to be
sued for damages, trade union leaders were also liable, and
trade union funds would not escape the consequences of an
illegal act.

Thomas Jones, who was deputy secretary of the cabinet
at the time, and so at the centre of events, wrote his own
account of the strike and his reflections on it which have
appeared in the second volume of his *Whitehall Diary*. He
showed how the way for the strike had been prepared by
the growing pressure of the big unions and the concentration
of power in a central executive, and how in 1925 a breath-
ing space was gained by the subsidy to maintain the miners'
wages and the setting up of a royal commission. The commission, under the chairmanship of Sir Herbert Samuel, a
Liberal and former cabinet minister, reported in March 1926
and recommended the ending of the subsidy, a reorganisation
of the mining industry, and, in return for agreement to re-
organise, a temporary reduction of wages. The government

was prepared to accept the report. But the owners were hostile to reorganisation proposals, while the government doubted how much reorganisation could help whereas the miners tended to exaggerate the economies it would bring. The miners' leaders, however, were determined to maintain their slogan "Not a penny off the pay, not a minute on the day". So there was deadlock. The leaders of both the miners and owners were obstructionists rather than negotiators; strikes and lock-outs were familiar, and were regarded as a normal way of settling differences. Indeed it was suggested that both sides felt that a few weeks' strike in the mining industry would make it easier for the men to accept inevitable reductions. On April 30th (Friday) negotiations broke down —the miners thinking that, at the last moment, the government would extend the subsidy beyond April and so avoid a reduction of wages. The miners were consistent right through—they would accept no reduction in wages.

The government stood firm, however, and the TUC took over negotiations, with the threat of a general strike. Over the Saturday and Sunday talks went on with the government, and great efforts for a settlement were made. Arthur Pugh, of the Iron and Steel Trades Confederation and Chairman of the General Council of the TUC and J. H. Thomas, struggled for moderation—while Bevin, Bromley, and Purcell were also active in the union discussions, which went on at TUC headquarters in Ecclestone Square all day and a large part of the night. Bevin worked hard for a settlement, but once the strike commenced he was one of the most energetic and efficient of those in control. It was touch-and-go until the last moment. Telegrams ordering the strike went out on the Saturday evening, May 1st. But even then the TUC did not break off contact with the government. On the Sunday, however, the government's attitude stiffened—it knew of the strike preparations and had heard of the *Daily Mail* incident. After a day of protracted meetings and comings and goings the cabinet decided to break off negotiations. Baldwin at No.

10 gave the news to the TUC leaders. They were astounded; it seemed that the government had seized on a minor incident as a pretext. Thus the nation stumbled into the general strike. The government—it had learnt its lesson when Baldwin had had to give way in 1925—had emergency measures ready, but the TUC had quickly to improvise. As Bevin's biographer, Alan Bullock, has put it. "After fifteen years' talk about a General Strike, Direct Action, and 'wielding the power of labour', the plain fact was that no plans of any sort existed."

The prime minister knew that the trade unionists and Labour leaders were uneasy about the strike, and was anxious to help them to make a retreat when the time came. But the strikers were remarkably united during the first week; meanwhile the government was able to maintain essential services. Behind the scenes, Sir Herbert Samuel was working as a voluntary mediator; his advances were well received by the TUC, and moderates began to see in him a means of saving face. At length the point was reached at which the strike had to be either carried to more extreme lengths or brought to an end. The TUC tried to interrupt the supply of food and to call out on strike the workers in further industries not yet involved. The prime minister made a conciliatory speech on the wireless. The union leaders discussed and argued, for hours and days. Their anxieties grew, and they were tired out. The TUC were unable to persuade the miners to accept Samuel's proposals for ending the strike, and at length decided to end the strike without the agreement of the miners. On May 12th the TUC leaders came to Downing Street and announced that the general strike was to be called off that day. To which Baldwin replied : "All I would say in answer to that is, I thank God for your decision." The general strike was indeed over. But, although Baldwin put forward new proposals for the mining industry, both miners and owners rejected them. The miners' strike went on, until at the end of the year they suffered defeat with wage reductions and further unemployment due to the loss of overseas markets.

Tom Jones's comments, written immediately after the memorable episode, had remarkable point and clarity and are of great value today in helping one to understand what had happened. First, he saw something of inevitability about it. "Few competent students of recent industrial history," he wrote, "will regret the General Strike. It, or something like it, 'had to come' in view of the temper of the most assertive elements in the trade union world." Yet at the same time, "the General Strike could not succeed because some of those who led it did not wholly believe in it and because few, if any, were prepared to go through with it to its logical conclusion—violence and revolution". So far as the actual stoppage of work went, "it manifested a most impressive trade union loyalty only equalled by the orderly behaviour of all concerned". Indeed the rank and file of the movement were taken by surprise when the strike was called off for they knew very little of the divisions of opinion and the personal jealousies among the leaders, and there was a disposition to condemn the TUC for betraying the miners. The miners themselves, however, began to lose sympathy when they showed their obstinacy in rejecting the Samuel proposals during the general strike and the government proposals immediately afterwards. In the day to day maintenance of essential services, certain modern technical developments had given the government an advantage—"the motorcar, aeroplane, and wireless were of immense value to the government". The same point was made, years later, by L. S. Amery, a member of the cabinet at the time. But behind everything was the character and reputation of Stanley Baldwin. As Tom Jones saw it—"The chief asset in keeping the country steadfast during the negotiations was the Prime Minister's reputation for fair dealing enhanced later by his sincere plea against malice and vindictiveness. His seeming weakness has been his strength. Had he yielded to the Die-hard influences he would have prolonged the strike by rallying the whole of Labour in defence of Trade Unionism. He was wise to give them the chance and he was enthusiastically supported in this course by the majority of the House of Commons."

The TUC had got out of an impossible situation, but it was difficult to see the general strike as anything other than a defeat for the Labour movement. Trade Union membership fell, and did not fully recover for nearly ten years. Union funds suffered heavy loss, as strike funds had been used up. And there was a loss of morale. The working class had made a remarkable show of strength and unity—but it had come to nothing; the men felt that the leaders had let them down. There was too, a certain amount of victimisation. "Never Again", perhaps, sums up the pessimistic attitude in trade union circles following the strike. Even while the strike was still in progress, Beatrice Webb in her diary forecast—and forecast correctly—"a day of terrible disillusionment" for the trade unions. "The failure of the General Strike of 1926 will be one of the most significant landmarks in the history of the British working-class. Future historians will, I think, regard it as the death-gasp of that pernicious doctrine of 'workers' control' of public affairs through the trade unions and by the method of direct action." With the failure of the general strike, something changed. The trade union movement was henceforth less militant. Direct action had been tried, and had proved unsuccessful. The trade union leaders had learnt that there were limits to their power. Taking industrial action on a nation-wide scale must have political and constitutional consequences, whether these were part of the original aim or not. Unless the trade union leaders were prepared to go the full length of revolution—and they were not—then the weapon of the general strike must be discarded.

Ramsay MacDonald, like Beatrice Webb, looked to a revival of parliamentary action through the Labour Party now that the general strike was over. Already in June, in *The Socialist Review*, he was remarkably outspoken in condemning it. "The General Strike is a weapon that cannot be wielded for industrial purposes. It is clumsy and ineffectual, it has no goal which, when reached, can be regarded as victory. . . . Some critics, who have responsibility for nothing, blame the General Council; some blame the miners. The real blame is with the General Strike itself and those who preached it without considering it and induced the workers to blunder into it. . . .

"I hope that the result will be a thorough reconsideration of trade-union tactics. . . . If the wonderful unity in the strike . . . would be shown in politics, Labour could solve the mining and similar difficulties through the ballot box."

There was danger of an open clash between Ramsay MacDonald and Bevin, between the political leader and the industrial. "I claim we had courage in calling that strike," Bevin wrote in a letter to Arthur Henderson, "in running it and in facing our job when it had to be called off, and this is not the time for the leader of the political party to be going around challenging the policy of the industrial side." And elsewhere, writing to one of the Labour intellectuals, Bevin described the strike as "a great, a tremendous thing . . . yet epoch-making events do not appeal to you as much as the muddy side of casting doubt and suspicion. That is and always has been my complaint against the so-called 'intelligentsia' and their 'superior' attitude of mind. Even inside the Labour movement, he alleged, "the 'superior class' attitude is always there in relation to the trade union leader who comes from the rank and file. We do not like your patronage. . . ." The bitterness is clear, and it reveals the latent animosity inside the movement between the socialist intellectuals and the working class trade unionists. But the quarrel was kept within bounds. And the bitterness passed. The Labour victory in 1929 showed how far relations had improved between the unions and the party.

The general strike, then, was not an attempt to impose socialism by force; it was not directed, as with Robert Owen and the trade unionists of 1833-4, towards a millennium and a new society. It had a limited, industrial objective : to help the miners in their struggle against the threat of lower wages and longer hours. But in calling out their full strength to help the miners, the TUC was using a desperate means of dealing with a desperate situation. For the situation of the miners was desperate; with increased competition, loss of markets, and consequent unemployment it taxed the wit of man, as exemplified in the Samuel Commission, to see how a reduction in wages could be avoided. And the reorganisation of the mining industry, advocated by the Commission, would have meant closing down uneconomic pits and reduction in the number of miners. When the TUC took over and threatened a general strike (though they did not use the term "general"), they believed and hoped that both miners and government would accept a settlement along the lines of the Samuel Commission. But the miners refused, and the government called the TUC's bluff and stood firm. The general strike followed, with no plan ready. When, after a week, the TUC saw the danger of violence ahead—a revolutionary abyss opening at their feet—they drew back, and called off the strike. This left the miners alone to struggle on to the bitterness of ultimate defeat. As far as the general strike itself went, however, it came to an end peaceably and without too much bitterness or victimisation. It was a very British ending to a characteristic British muddle. Although some of the extremists in the Labour movement were, no doubt, still convinced that a great revolutionary opportunity had been lost, the majority accepted the lesson of defeat and turned back to the search for socialism by parliamentary means.

11. The Russian Influence

SOVIET RUSSIA—EXAMPLE or warning, which was it to be? From the beginning the attitude of British socialists was ambivalent to a high degree. The foundation, at last, of a socialist society created by the working class was eminently attractive; but, at the same time, what was democratic, what was liberal, what was based in the religious tradition, what, in effect, was British, was antagonised and repelled, not once only, but again and again, as the development of modern Russia proceeded from 1917 onwards.

The Leeds conference, in June 1917, had given a welcome to revolution in Russia. The conference of twelve hundred represented various socialistic societies, the LLP, Labour Party local groups, trade unions, and trades councils, among the delegates were Ramsay MacDonald, Snowden, Tom Mann, Sylvia Pankhurst, Bevin, Gallacher and Maxton, and Bertrand Russell. The Leeds meeting has been described by an American historian as "one of the great anomalies in British Labour experience". It was left wing inspired, yet the future moderates Ramsay MacDonald and Snowden were temporarily carried away. Only Bevin spoke out as a patriot, and with a note of scepticism, among the pacifists and idealistic revolutionaries. The conference was, as Alan Bullock well describes it, "a preview of the British Left between the wars, anarchical, Utopian, already fascinated by and profoundly ignorant of Russian experience". But change was in the air. The conference supported a move to set up, on the Russian model, workers' and soldiers' councils. A few days later the left wing groups produced a *New Charter for the Workers*, a draft programme advocating conscription of wealth, state ownership of industry with management by the workers, and self-government for soldiers and sailors in the services. Nothing happened, yet the Russian Revolution indicated a change of attitude which affected people all over Europe. Men would never again return to the old conditions before the war. The immediate post-war years were marked by serious industrial conflict, and the workers were looking for fundamental, socialist policies. They wanted nationalisation of mines, railways, and land, a capital levy, and an end to poverty and class distinctions. Soviet Russia took on a symbolic character : for the workers it represented the achievement—real or imagined—of their aspirations, for the upper and middle class it stood for all they feared in the tyranny of the mob. And so Left and Right took sides whenever Russia figured in international affairs, and it was not surprising that Labour condemned the intervention of Allied troops in the Russian Civil War (the Allies had sought to maintain a Russian front against Germany when the Bolsheviks took Russia out of the war) and sprang to the defence of the Soviet Government when war broke out in 1920 between Russia and Poland. British dockers refused to ship arms destined for Poland. When Russian armies threatened Warsaw, British government opinion feared an extension of communism into the heart of Europe, but Labour regarded any offer of aid from the West as a conservative attempt to help the Poles to defeat the Red Army.

From the Revolution onwards there was naturally an especial interest in the fortunes of Soviet Russia, an interest which was felt in Britain especially by socialists but also by others. There was also ignorance—and mystery. Russia was far away, it was difficult to visit it, and Russians were not allowed to travel abroad. The interest in Russia rose or fell with circumstances. The Revolution itself had aroused revolutionary enthusiasm abroad; then the consequent horrors and savagery of the civil war caused a reaction, and the fears and hatreds were still strong at the time of the first Labour Government when the proposed trade treaty and the Zinoviev letter brought its downfall; there was less concern with Russia during the middle and late 1920s when there was a degree of European recovery; then the world economic slump which, after the Wall Street crash in the autumn of 1929, set in in the early 1930s, brought Russia back once more into the picture—capitalism appeared to be in collapse, and people began to wonder if, after all, Soviet communism might not indicate an alternative; the tyranny of Stalin with its treason trials and purges led to renewed suspicions and the agreement with Nazi Germany in 1939 and the Russian attack on Finland caused a strong revulsion of feeling against Russia; and this, in turn, was followed by a new enthusiasm for our Russian ally, with Hitler's invasion in 1941.

Every movement has its lunatic fringe, and this was certainly true of the socialist movement in its attitude to Soviet Russia. The Communist Party in Russia, that is to say, the Russian Government, and the Third International created by Russia were both committed to the idea of world revolution. But the socialist lunatic fringe in Britain were blind to the threat this meant to their own country—or if not blind, then they welcomed it—and in their speeches and publications represented Russia as a kind of socialist paradise, where all the disadvantages of capitalism had been overcome and a new society established in a brave new world. Thus a member of Nottingham Labour Party, who visited Russia in 1931, declared: "They have enthroned and dignified labour and abolished unnecessary toil. They are aiming at a Socialist paradise, with complete equality of the sexes, a real land of hope and glory. It is the workers' first fatherland, not a speculator's heaven. A good standard of life is guaranteed in exchange for good citizenship". Then there was the illustrated *Russia To-day* published by the "Friends of the Soviet Union"—"Where are we today? Ten times worse off than ten years ago! All our sacrifices have been to help the profit-mongers .... The Russian workers' sacrifices have brought them gigantic socialist successes and the dawn of a new era." John Strachey, a prolific left-wing writer and a future Labour minister, found no difficulty in

accepting that "the Soviet Union is a working-class dictatorship", and he suggested communism as a road for others to
follow. In *The Coming Struggle for Power* he wrote : "The
coming of communism can alone render our problems
soluble. A working-class dictatorship can alone open the way
to communism." Another uncritical admirer of the Soviet
Union was Fred Jowett, who had held office in the first
Labour Cabinet, and who apparently regarded Russia as a
good democratic country. "I have always held the view,"
he said, "that it was a great mistake to describe the system
of government established by Lenin and his Party in Russia
as a dictatorship ... the franchise in Russia probably gives
votes to a greater proportion of the population than in any
country in Europe, or possibly, in the world."

During the 1920s the General Council of the TUC and
the All-Russian Central Council of Trade Unions exchanged
delegations, speeches were made, and fraternal greetings
offered. In the 1930s visits to Russia became comparatively
common; the Russians were in need of foreign currency
for purchases abroad, and had established an official tourist
agency—Intourist—to bring foreigners to Russia, though
Russians themselves were not allowed to leave their country.
All kinds of people visited Russia—during the depression
unemployed from England and America sought work there,
and there were tourists with enquiring minds. Bernard Shaw
visited Russia in 1931 and was convinced that Stalin could
not understand how people could be so foolish as not to see
the benefit of the Communist system. In 1932 the Webbs
set out on their journey to what seemed to some a promised
land, and Mr Harold Macmillan, Conservative MP and
future premier, made a visit; Walter Citrine, general secretary of the TUC was there in 1925 and again in 1935, and
published his book the following year, *I Search for Truth in
Russia*. Maurice Dobb, the left-wing Cambridge economist,
wrote his *Russia To-day and To-morrow* in 1932, and about
the same time three Labour MPs, Aneurin Bevan, John

Strachey, and G. Strauss wrote *What we saw in Russia.*
H. G. Wells had a conversation with Stalin in Moscow
which was reproduced in the pages of *The New Statesman
and Nation* in 1934, and the questions raised were taken up
and discussed in subsequent issues by Bernard Shaw and
J. M. Keynes. The Durham Miners' Association sent a party
to Soviet Russia in 1936 and they published their report, *A
Visit to Russia*, in the following year. There were many
more. Strachey's *Coming Struggle for Power* analysed the
features of decay and forecast the dissolution of the capitalist
system. The interest in Soviet Russia was intense.

At least from 1933 onwards Hitler began to overshadow
Europe, especially when the Spanish Civil War (1936-9)
excited intense feeling among progressive people everywhere.
There were moves for a Popular Front, of socialists, communists, liberals, and for bringing Britain, France, and
Russia together against the Nazi menace. One manifestation
of this new feeling was the Left Book Club run by Victor
Gollancz, which put out a flood of books attacking Fascism
and capitalism.

A careful and balanced observer among the Labour
visitors to Russia was Walter Citrine, later Lord Citrine.
Starting out with what was a quite usual socialist enthusiasm
for Russia, his visits to that country taught him caution.
Describing his attitude in the early 1920s he wrote: "I had
been enthused by Lenin's picture of an electric republic,
organised on such lines as would ensure to every citizen,
however humble, the advantages of a planned economy and
the blessings of a modern civilisation. I had read eagerly of
the immense strides in economic reconstruction which were
rapidly enabling the Soviet Union to recover from the effects
of the Civil War. True, I had read something of the reluctance of the peasantry to give up their individualistic form
of agriculture, but I had little doubt that this was a transient
difficulty which would be resolved in due course". He went
on to explain how his enthusiasm brushed aside considerations

which were less favourable. "I accepted almost at its face value, without critical reservations, practically everything which emanated from Russian official sources. I entirely disbelieved the stories which appeared occasionally of the quarrels between the Communist leaders, particularly Lenin and Trotsky, and attributed these to the biased capitalist Press. I was convinced that our newspapers simply couldn't tell the truth about events in the Soviet Union."

About the fatal disagreements among the Russian leaders, Citrine was later to have personal experience. Mikhail Tomsky came to England as a trade union delegate, he looked after Citrine on his early visit to Russia, and Citrine got to know him well. During the treason trials of 1936 Tomsky shot himself rather than face arrest—"driven to his death by the calumnies and suspicions of the men who, a few years before, had sent him proudly as their leader to the British Trades Union Congress at Scarborough".

On his first visit Citrine was surprised, as a British trade unionist, to find that the Russian trade unions had no independence but were part of the government organisation and subordinate to the Communist Party. He was also horrified both by the beggars he saw at railway stations, and, even more, by the miserable crowd of ragged people, old men, women, and children, he saw hiding themselves in a pile of straw on a cold night near the Bolshoi Theatre. "This is one of Russia's problems, comrade," said his guide. "We can do nothing about it."

On his second visit in 1935, he saw how bad economic conditions were, so different from what the Russian enthusiasts at home were saying—clothes and shoes were shoddy, there was serious shortage of housing and great overcrowding, and building work was poor. Food was very dear. He knew, of course, the Russian plea that they were having to spend a large part of their income on military defence against the danger of attack by fascist powers. He felt sometimes that he was being shown only the new show houses, whereas when he insisted on going off on his own, he found the most dreadful hovels. He realised that the propagandists were at fault. "It is not so much what the Russians themselves claim," he wrote, "as what their insistent propagandists claim for them. They give the impression that Russia is rapidly becoming a workers' paradise, with better conditions than exist anywhere else. It is only when they are brought face to face with actualities that they admit conditions are not as they should be."

What most worried Citrine, however, was the ruthless character of the communist dictatorship in Russia, and the trials and many executions of the years 1936, 1937, and 1938. Trotsky was already in exile, and by these purges Stalin rid himself of most of the 'Old Bolsheviks' who, with Lenin, had made the revolution. The list read like a communist *Who's Who*—Zinoviev, Kamenev, Bukharin, Radek, Rykov, Marchal Tukhachevsky and seven generals, and hundreds of the lesser known. These men were accused of treachery, fascism, counter-revolution, they were denounced as fascist dogs—yet until recently they had been, with Stalin, the governors of Russia. When Citrine and other members of the socialist international organisations appealed to the Soviet government for proper legal defence for Zinoviev they met a torrent of abuse calling them "allies of the Gestapo and accomplices of fascism". To what a pass socialism in Russia had come! "Meanwhile," as Citrine pointed out, "the opponents of socialism the world over exult at what they are pleased to describe as the 'end of socialism'. But what is vaunted as socialism in Russia, with its emphasis on an unsatisfying materialism, and its reckless waste of human life in the achievement of the ends decreed by the State, is something which British socialists, brought up on the precepts of Charles Kingsley, John Ruskin, William Morris, Edward Carpenter, Keir Hardie and others, cannot recognise as having any relation to those higher ethical and moral principles, the realisation of which has been the hope and

aspiration of millions of socialists throughout the world."
Another socialist—Evan Durbin—showed considerable
courage in comparing the horrors in Soviet Russia with
those in Nazi Germany.

Thus Citrine saw clearly enough the challenge to western
socialist principles in Soviet practice. On the other hand the
Webbs, the founders of Fabian socialism, were pathetic
in their determination to think that everything was right in
Soviet Russia. By the time they fell for Russia they were
famous people. Sidney had been in each of the Labour
Cabinets, and had become Lord Passfield, though Beatrice
refused to use the title. Their partnership had produced
many solid volumes on British social institutions, and they
were turning at last to a serious study of the Russian system
—a study which Bernard Shaw praised uncritically in the
later years of the war when Soviet Russia was our ally. Yet
how little Shaw knew about Russia or Beatrice Webb, for
that matter! Before the book was published, the Webbs
visited Russia in the early summer of 1932—"with a draft
of their foregone conclusions (the result of months of
scientific investigation) safely stowed in their luggage", as
Kitty Muggeridge, the niece of Beatrice, described it in her
biography of her aunt. The picture she draws of the Webbs
is a sad one : at the end of their lives, socialism no nearer
after two Labour Governments, losing faith in the inevitability of gradualness (as Beatrice noted in her diary)—"the
two disillusioned old Fabians, with a combined age of one
hundred and forty-seven, steamed out of the port of London
with renewed hope, Beatrice fervently praying that the
Communist experiment would turn out to be a success".

In Leningrad they had a royal reception on the quay and
stayed in a luxury hotel. But Kitty Muggeridge, who had
travelled out by Intourist and was staying at a hostel,
sampled the food in a workers' restaurant. She remarked
that you could eat better on the dole at home. But Beatrice
would not hear of it. Leningrad and Moscow were passable,

but travelling south on the Volga steamer Beatrice found a
bug (only one—she was lucky!). Conditions were uncom-
fortable, and Beatrice fell ill. But in spite of famine conditions, they were impressed—by the new factories, the
advance of education, the enthusiasm of the new governing
class. They came back to England with a firm impression
of the wonders of Russia, and it seemed to them more than
ever that the socialist leaders at home lacked the revolutionary spirit. They got busy with the actual writing of their
book, *Soviet Russia, A New Civilisation?* Which appeared
in 1935. Later, more assured, they dispensed with the
question mark in the editions of 1937 and later. They were
content to have their chapters read and checked by the
Russian Embassy. And they used their "official" figures in
an argument with Walter Citrine. Meanwhile reports from
Russia were discouraging. The newspapers at home were
full of the trial in Moscow of British engineers accused of
sabotage, and there were accounts of failures on the collective farms and of food shortages amounting almost to
famine. Malcolm Muggeridge, who had gone to Russia for
the *Manchester Guardian*, returned disillusioned. Like so
many young men of the time he had been struck by the
failure of capitalism in the world slump, and had wondered
if Russian communism could be the answer. His satire
Winter in Moscow, which appeared in 1934, recorded his
disapproval. But he did not shake his redoubtable aunt.
At length, when the Webbs' book was finished they asked
a fundamental question, and gave their own answer to it:
"Will this new civilisation with its abandon of the incentive
of profit-making, its extinction of unemployment, its planned
production for community consumption, and the consequent
liquidation of the landlord and the capitalist, spread to other
countries? Our own reply is: 'Yes, it will.' Though, how,
when, and where must be in doubt."

So just as Stalin's cruel reign of terror was setting in, the
Webbs were able to believe that all was well. Or did they?

They did, in fact, suggest that their admiration for Russia might be due to old age—"Old people often fall in love in extraordinary and ridiculous ways . . . we feel it more dignified to have fallen in love with Soviet Communism". And we are told, "the Webbs like everyone else in the late thirties, were horrified by Stalin's purges".

Yet their book put forward a powerful case for Soviet Russia—powerful because of the Webbs' established reputation as social investigators. They examined the Soviet constitution, and dismissed the charge that Stalin was a dictator. "Stalin is . . . not in the least a dictator," they affirmed, and they reached this confident conclusion because he was not mentioned "by the constitution"; and "he appears to be free from any desire to act as a dictator". His position or office, by which he earns his living and to which he owes his predominant position, was that of secretary of the Communist Party. Yet they accepted that Stalin "a national leader so persistently boosted, and so generally admired, has, in fact, become irremovable against his will . . . . He will, therefore, remain in his great position of leadership so long as he wishes to do so". Not a dictator, then, according to the constitution, but nevertheless a leader whose position rests upon his own will! Again, they asked the question: "Is the Party a Dictator?" And here they had to admit that it had great authority. As Stalin had written: "In the Soviet Union . . . no important political or organisational problem is ever decided by our Soviets and other mass organisations, without directives from our Party. In this sense, we may say that the dictatorship of the proletariat is substantially the dictatorship of the Party". After this even the Webbs had to say—although in parentheses—"How the Bolsheviks do love the word dictatorship!" But the Webbs did not love the word. And a few sentences further on, writing of the potent influence of the Communist Party, they said: "the term dictatorship is surely a misnomer for this untiring corporate institution". They also asked the question:

"Is the USSR an autocracy?" And they answered: "the Government of the USSR is ... actually less of an autocracy or a dictatorship than many a parliamentary cabinet". Of this political democracy one of the outstanding features was its racial equality. In a short publication, issued during the war, and based on the Soviet constitution of 1936, Beatrice was even more definite about Russia not being a dictatorship, and she went on to explain and defend the one-party system in Russia (the Communist Party stands alone and no opposition party is allowed)—not an easy task if democracy means any real freedom of choice.

When they went on to deal with the economic side of Russian life they were on surer ground. No one could dispute that in Soviet Russia there had been a transference of the ownership and control of industry and agriculture from private hands to the state on a scale never before known in history. This was the unique feature of the Russian experiment—the putting into practice of socialism. The creation and development of state industries, the organisation of agriculture by means of thousands of collective farms and a number of state farms, and the establishment of a planning department (*Gosplan*) which produced the successive Five-Year plans from 1928 onwards, these were its main features. The fundamental transformation of the social order—the substitution of planned production for community consumption, instead of the capitalist profit-making of so-called 'Western Civilisation'—seemed a change for the better, conducive to the progress of humanity to higher levels of health and happiness, virtue and wisdom, and constituting a new civilisation. Soviet statesmen were, the Webbs thought, aiming at "erecting a shining example of socialism in a single country, which can be imitated elsewhere".

But the dilemma remained for the plain man, for the plain member of the British Labour Party. Whatever the Webbs said about Soviet Russia, however plausible they could make it all sound in theory, Soviet Russia was not like

that. Too many other people had been to Russia, and seen
for themselves. If one accepted the socialist policy of public
ownership and control, must one accept also the methods
of Stalin's dictatorship? If one did, then one got something
which, as Citrine had pointed out, was not the kind of
socialism which the socialists of Britain wanted. And if one
said that the development of Soviet Russia was determined
by its circumstances—by the savagery, ignorance, autocracy
of the past, that by titanic struggles and a dreadful cost in
human life the Communists were, in a different way, doing
what Western countries had done earlier in their own
Industrial Revolutions, then one had to admit that Russia
was at an earlier stage than the West, that the West had
moved on, and that what Russia was doing was not, after
all, something which the West could take over as a solution
for its own problems.

How wrong-headed can one be, and get away with it?
The Webbs' book won considerable acclaim. They were the
experts. They were—and so regarded themselves, as Kitty
Muggeridge points out—brilliant publicists. Here was the
element of tragedy. Great and profound thinkers as they
were, they were growing old, and were out of their depths
when dealing with Soviet Russia—just as Neville Chamber-
lain (with whose father Beatrice had once been half in love)
was an outstanding minister of health but quite unable to
cope with Hitler. "For eminent services to social and political
science", Sidney Webb received the Order of Merit. In
1947, after a letter by Bernard Shaw to *The Times*, the
ashes of Sidney and Beatrice were buried in Westminster
Abbey. This was when the post-war socialist government was
in power—the first socialist government to be actually in
power in Britain and the first to introduce any socialism.
There were over two hundred Fabians in the House of
Commons and ten in the cabinet. It was the heyday of
British socialism.

PART IV

12. The Labour Governments of Attlee and Wilson

THE HEYDAY OF Socialism? Indeed, it was. For with the Second World War everything changed again. The Labour Party which had suffered debacle in 1931, achieved its greatest electoral victory only fourteen years later. In July 1945 the Labour Party won a majority in parliament for the first time. Socialists felt that at last the new age was coming. As it seemed to Hugh Dalton, in the words of Edward Carpenter's socialist hymn: "England is risen and the day is here". And with its victory came a safe full-term five years office. With 393 Labour members, it had a majority of 146 over all other parties; it polled approximately twelve million votes against ten million for the Conservatives, and two and a quarter million for the Liberals. The Labour Party elected in 1945 was in a sense a new party. Many of its members, about two-thirds, had never before been in parliament—rather than working class they were middle class professional people, lawyers, journalists, doctors, teachers and university lecturers. Under the new prime minister, Clement Attlee who had been to Public School and to Oxford, the government introduced a notable degree of socialism, more than the working class leaders had done, and indeed the only socialism to be introduced by Labour governments either before or after the war. The Second World War, like the First, brought opportunity to the

Labour Party, but this time in a more spectacular way.

The Labour leaders had taken a prominent part in Churchill's wartime coalition. Attlee and Greenwood were members of the war cabinet, and Bevin, Morrison, Dalton and Alexander held posts in the Government. Bevin later joined the war cabinet, and Attlee became deputy premier. Labour, therefore, shared responsibility for the conduct of the war, and shared also in the triumph when victory was won. There was a revival also of belief in Labour's policy, for planning was characteristic of the conduct of the war. The war had been won by centralised state planning in the military, economic, and social spheres; an immense war effort under government control had resulted in the training, clothing, feeding, and movement of millions of men and women in the services, and at home a vast production of armaments had been organised, and the workers maintained and fed. In spite of the bombing, the peacetime evils of unemployment, poverty, and malnutrition virtually disappeared. To many this must have appeared as a vindication of Labour's policy of state ownership and control. If so much could be achieved in wartime by planning, why, it was asked, could it not be done also in peacetime. Along with this, went the more generalised determination—as in the First World War—to create a better world after the war. The victories of the Red Army aroused enthusiasm for Soviet Russia; the excesses of the pre-war period were quickly forgotten, and the public generally was not yet aware of the difficulties the British Government was already having with the Russians. Indeed, it seemed that the organisation of the Russian war effort was another triumph for the socialist policy of state planning. Even in capitalist America, Roosevelt had introduced the New Deal policy of public works and assistance during the depression, and under his leadership the United States produced a vast and rapidly organised war effort both in the West and in the Far East. In a sense, the Second World War saved socialism—temporarily. The belief in wartime state planning gave it a new lease of life, by obscuring the new Keynesian techniques of economic control (by budgetary and credit policy rather than physical means) which were coming into operation; it also blinded one to the fact that in wartime a government can do things it cannot do in peacetime, and that in wartime people will work harder, accept burdens, and put up with rationing and controls.

Conditions, then, were favourable in 1945 for the return of a Labour government, though the extent of these favourable conditions was not realised at the time. Attlee and his colleagues were surprised by the Labour victory, and they do not appear to have been thinking of a complete transformation of the social system such as earlier socialist manifestos had put forward. Yet the Labour Party was committed to a socialist policy. Reports of its reconstruction committee had recommended nationalisation of mining, transport, gas, and electricity, and the annual conference of 1944 passed resolutions advocating "the transfer to the state of power to direct the policy of our main industries, services, and financial institutions". Mr Shinwell declared that "the Socialist policy of the Labour Party remains unchanged". Yet the position was that while active socialists were pressing socialist motions on the conference, the executive was cautious.

The Labour Party programme, on which the election was fought after the wartime coalition was brought to an end, was published in April 1945. *Let Us face the Future* stated that the Labour Party "is a Socialist Party, and proud of it. Its ultimate purpose at home is the establishment of the Socialist Commonwealth of Great Britain—free, democratic, efficient, progressive, public-spirited, its material resources organised in the service of the British people". The programme, however, struck a note of caution—"Socialism cannot come overnight, as the product of a week-end revolution. The members of the Labour Party, like the

British people, are practical-minded men and women". The programme also differentiated between "basic industries ripe and over-ripe for public ownership and management", "big industries not yet ripe for public ownership", and "many smaller businesses rendering good service which can be left to go on with their useful work"—all reminiscent of Mr Douglas Jay's book in 1937, and meaning that a large part of private industry would not come under nationalisation. The party chairman, Harold Laski, however, described the election as a "straight fight . . . a fight between private enter-prise now expressed as monopoly capitalism and socialism".

But in sober fact, the Labour government did carry out a remarkable series of changes along socialist lines, and these changes sprang from the socialist policy of *Let Us face the Future*. As an American writer has indicated, "to an extent unprecedented in British political history the legislation of a Government was dictated by a party program". Or, as Herbert Morrison put it : "It was on the basis of this policy document that the majority Labour Government set about shaping both its legislative programme and its work of administration" and it acted with the intention of seeking "to implement the legislative aspects of *Let Us face the Future* within the lifetime of a single Parliament". This was what the Government did. For to meet each of the principal pledges made in the programme the Government passed a law. The programme promised to nationalise the Bank of England, the fuel and power industries, inland trans-port (road, railway, air, and canal), and the iron and steel industry. These promises were fulfilled in seven statutes: the Bank of England Act (1946), the Coal Industry Nationalisa-tion Act (1946) the Civil Aviation Act (1946), the Electricity Act (1947), the Transport Act (1947), the Gas Act (1948), and the Iron and Steel Act (1949), though this measure was to have a chequered history.

In other spheres also, notably land and taxation, the Government tried to follow a socialistic policy of extending public control over available resources for the public good. The Town and Country Planning Act of 1947 aimed at securing to the public the financial benefit to be derived from the development of land, by restricting the owner's interest to the existing use of the land. The Agriculture Act of the same year continued and extended a system of assuring markets and guaranteeing prices to farmers, a system which went back to the marketing boards of the Labour government in 1931 or even to the sugar-beet subsidy of the 1920s. In 1948 another measure was directed against monopolies and restrictive practices. At the same time the government carried over from wartime a sharply progressive taxation, and, to facilitate the transition from war to peace, it passed the Supplies and Services (Transitional Powers) Act of 1945 which enabled it to use many of the wide powers that government had employed in wartime. And behind it all the government had always in mind the prime necessity, in both its direct policy of socialism by nationalisation and in its use of financial machinery, of maintaining full employment.

Then there was the "Welfare State"—a term which came later into general use to describe the social activities of the state—for the government carried out a pledge to introduce great programmes of social services. Three Acts were passed in 1946. The National Insurance Act consolidated and extended existing social insurance, which became widely comprehensive. Everyone was to pay contributions into a state fund which would provide financial help to the sick, unemployed, bereaved women and children, and the aged. The National Assistance Act covered anyone who was not provided for, or not sufficiently provided for, under national insurance. The National Health Service Act provided free medical and dental treatment, and free hospital treatment when necessary; it also provided free medicine, dentures, and spectacles—though, because of the heavy cost, some charges were later on introduced. In addition, attention was given to the improvement of child welfare services in the Children Act of 1948, while in trying to provide good family accommodation for all the government passed Housing Acts in 1946 and 1949 and the Rent Control Act of 1949.

What Labour achieved, was achieved in conditions of great difficulty. Just as after the First World War, immense and intractable problems faced the government. But whereas in the first instance war was followed by many years of depression, industrial unrest and unemployment, in the second, serious unrest and unemployment were avoided and after an early period of restrictions and austerity the country entered one marked by full employment and affluence. Whereas in the thirties the key notes had been the dole and the means test, in the late forties and the fifties they were the welfare state and the affluent society. Indeed it is now difficult, twenty-five years after the war, to recall the forbidding circumstances amid which Labour took office. The new government faced a battle both for economic recovery and for social reconstruction. There was the analogy of Dunkirk—Britain had experienced a miraculous escape from the German armies, and had at length been saved only by the fact that she found powerful allies, whereas in 1945 she faced the appalling difficulties of rebuilding her foreign trade and was barely saved from disaster by the American loan and later by Marshall Aid. Attlee had still in 1947 to describe Britain's economic position in grim terms. The vast war effort had placed an enormous burden on the British economy; the war had disrupted the economic system. But by 1949, Sir Stafford Cripps, the chancellor of the exchequer, could report that "not only have we travelled a long way on the road to economic recovery, but we have, in addition, carried through, and paid and provided for, the greatest programme of social services ever undertaken in any country in so short a period of time, while at the same time surpassing all previous records for exports and capital investment at home". "Four years of hard work and of solid achievements", James Griffiths, the Labour Party chairman as well as a minister in the government, put it. Austerity continued; there was no prospect of tax relief, and defence expenditure was high because of fear of Russia and the war in Korea. Yet in spite of her wartime losses—bomb damage, deterioration of buildings and equipment, the destruction of shipping, a huge public debt, and vast expenditure overseas together with loss of overseas investments—Britain was recovering.

The long-term problem was the gap between Britain's exports and imports—how the country could export more and pay for its necessary imports. But the Labour government had also its periods of internal crisis, arising when circumstances became acute or when the dissatisfaction of its own left-wingers reached bursting point. In November 1946 the left-wing group revolted over foreign affairs—it disliked Bevin's foreign policy—but to no avail. The long and bitter winter of 1946-47 saw a fuel crisis in February— electricity consumption mounted rapidly, coal supplies were running down. Power cuts were frequent, factories were having to stop production. There was a sterling crisis in July and August 1947, and the government had to suspend convertibility. In September 1949 the pound was devalued, and, towards the end of the same year, the East African groundnut project collapsed. But, in spite of these crises and the tensions set up as a result inside the cabinet and the party, the government went on its way.

And all the time the Attlee administration had to deal, not only with the ordinary, every-day work of government, but also with a number of issues of the first importance, issues of a kind which many governments in normal circumstances would never have to face. The government had to make a peace settlement with the enemy powers, it had to meet the Cold War forced on the West by Soviet Russia, and it had to conduct the critical, sometimes tragic, negotiations and changes which, starting with the independence of India and Pakistan in 1947, led to the transformation of the old British Empire into the Commonwealth of today. When all these things are borne in mind the Attlee Government can be regarded as one of the most important in our history—although not yet, because so recent, fully treated by historians. Attlee himself could say with justice that his government had carried out the programme which he had put before the electorate in 1945, and Herbert Morrison could claim with reason that the Government had achieved "the most extensive and significant legislative programme in the history of our great Parliament". Certainly it was the greatest implementation of a socialist programme, and curiously it was the last.

The Labour government had made possible a transition from a capitalist to what was at least partly a socialist state; it introduced what has been called a mixed economy. It laid foundations which later governments, Conservative ones, would accept. Nevertheless, people tired of Labour administration. There were many shortages, and many things were still rationed. Not unnaturally rationing and the acute housing shortage were much more resented in peacetime than in wartime. "Spivs" began to operate a black market. Such things contributed to the decline in popularity of the government. In the election of 1950 it gained an overall majority of six, and struggled on. But the government itself appeared to have run out of inspiration and of fight. In 1951 another election gave the Conservatives a small majority—actually the total votes were very close, with Labour very slightly ahead. But this was the beginning of a long period of Conservative government—they greatly improved their position in 1955—and Conservative governments were in power until 1964.

These years were very difficult ones for the Labour Party. The Conservatives did not, as many Labour people expected, prove a disastrous alternative to Labour. Conservatives, too, had come to understand that full employment and the welfare state must be maintained. Indeed it was the National Government of Churchill which had published in 1944 the White Paper recommending that the government should be responsible for maintaining a high level of employment. Affluence continued. One Conservative premier, Harold Macmillan, was able to assure the people that they had "never had it so good". Nor did a period in opposition restore the vitality of the Labour Party, for it suffered a period of crisis, both as to its policy and as to its leadership.

The crises centred on the traditional Labour policy of socialism, and it saw the virtual disappearance of socialism as a policy. The older men, like Herbert Morrison, tended to think that the work of socialism was done, and were now in favour of consolidation and moderation. And the very experience of the Labour government of 1945 had led to a shift of emphasis in policy from planning and actual physical controls to controls by means of financial policy—a development forecast already in Mr Jay's book in 1937. In any case the Labour Party had long been moving away from its working class image. Attlee had been educated at Haileybury and Oxford—though he looked like Lenin and, as far as practical results went, was the best socialist of the lot; then there were Dalton, Eton and King's, Cambridge, and Sir Stafford Cripps, Winchester and London University. And a new generation was coming to the top, from Winchester and New College, Oxford, Hugh Gaitskell, Douglas Jay, R. H. S. Crossman, and the Hon. Francis Pakenham, Eton and New College. When, after Labour's defeat in the General Election of 1955, Attlee resigned the leadership of the Party, Gaitskell was elected leader by a large majority over Bevan and Morrison. This was a clear victory by an intellectual and a revisionist (as to Labour's long established basic policies) over both the Left as represented by Bevan, and the older—but by now—moderate and conservative section of the party. The *Economist* declared that the new leader's task was "to turn his back on Keir Hardie". No longer was the Labour Party engaged in a bitter struggle against hard-faced capitalists, grinding poverty and crime, but rather in a struggle for more wealth, leisure, and equal opportunity.

Gaitskell's leadership of the Labour Party meant that socialism—at least, socialism as formerly interpreted—was pushed into the background. It is possible, even for members of the same party, either to regret or to welcome this; some regret the disappearance of the socialist principle, others maintain that Gaitskell saved the party from suicidal tendencies and made it fit once more to form a government. But it was a long time before Labour's come back. In the 1959 general election Labour suffered its third successive defeat, and after it Gaitskell set himself more definitely to work at the revision of Labour's traditional policy of socialism. He found his supporters among the intellectuals, Douglas Jay, Crosland, Roy Jenkins and Patrick Gordon Walker. Jay, whose revisionist attitude dated back to the 1930s or perhaps, to even earlier Liberal sympathies, was outspoken. He maintained, after the election, that "we should say that we accept the decision of the electorate and would in future propose no further nationalisation". He also felt that the close association with the old working classes was losing its reality in the new affluent society—"we are," he put it, "in danger of fighting under the label of a class that no longer exists".

So it was that Gaitskell undertook in 1959-60 to change or modify Clause IV of the Labour Party Constitution which committed the party to "the common ownership of the means of production, distribution, and exchange". This clause he saw as an obstacle to Labour electoral success. Nationally, the voting strength was fairly equally divided between Labour and Conservative. There was a kind of "middle ground", an uncommitted body of voters which could turn the scale, and these voters were likely to be repelled by any such doctrinaire commitment. He failed to persuade the Labour Party conference, and the constitution remained unchanged. But the very fact that the leader of the party was known not to accept wholeheartedly the policy of socialism deprived it of its importance. It was now something of sentimental value only. James Griffiths put the issue clearly, later on, when he attributed Gaitskell's attack on Clause IV to his integrity of character. "We do not now intend to carry this out fully" was the leader's view, and hence the clause should be changed. Yet, as Griffiths pointed out, to men of his generation the clause was an article of faith. His generation, however, was passing, and it was clear that the Labour Party was changing, was ceasing to be a socialist party, and was becoming a party without ideological attachment.

But Gaitskell died prematurely in 1963, and Labour lost its leader. Yet Dr Stephen Haseler, who has investigated very carefully Gaitskell's part in re-creating the Labour Party, says that "his greatest achievement was to prepare Labour for Government and to give it clear and definite leadership during the long years in opposition". From this Harold Wilson, the new leader, would benefit, for "Labour's credibility as a responsible and non-doctrinaire alternative government in the election of 1964 rested largely upon Gaitskell's legacy". As to socialism, Dr Haseler underlines that "What is certain is the fact that Gaitskell's headlong assault upon Clause IV, the principal article of faith since 1918, was so traumatic that its effects are still with us. It remains one of the most explosive episodes in Labour's long search for its true identity". And what is equally certain, for it is now a matter of history, is that the subsequent Labour government of Harold Wilson was no more socialist than Gaitskell's would have been.

In 1964 the Labour Party won the election with an overall majority of four; in 1966 it won a secure position with a majority of ninety-seven. The new prime minister, Harold

Wilson, had a middle-class background; he went to a grammar school, had a brilliant academic record at Oxford, afterwards teaching there as a don. His government faced a difficult and complex situation, many problems and growing violence overseas, in the Commonwealth, and later in Northern Ireland. At home economic crisis threatened, with growing difficulty about the balance of payments, a difficulty met by "Stop-Go" expedients and then by devaluation of the pound. The last attempt at any kind of centralised state planning was the National Plan published in September 1965, which aimed at 25 per cent increase in our national production in order to correct the balance of payments and pay our debts. But the plan was soon forgotten as the economic position grew worse. Labour also tried to reform the House of Lords and to curb strikes, but met with failure. Of socialism, there was no sign. In the general election of 1970 the Labour Party was defeated. The Labour manifesto, *Now Britain's strong let's make it great to live in,* made no mention of the word socialism.

Indeed a new problem now faced, not only a Labour government, but any government—the position of the trade unions in the state. The Second World War had again deeply involved the unions with the government in the task of winning the war, and the results lasted longer than on the first occasion. The Labour government of 1945 was successful in persuading the unions to accept a policy of voluntary wage restraint to keep prices stable at home and to encourage the all-important exports. Even under the Conservatives from 1951 onwards, the unions remained remarkably quiescent, and satisfied with the machinery of joint consultation. The old militancy began to seem a thing of the past. Yet their numbers were very great; membership had risen from six millions in 1938 to nearly nine and a half millions in 1951, and the trade unions had not—and would not—abandon their traditional policy of freedom of action in wage bargaining. By the middle 1950s the nation and the unions

themselves were troubled by an increasing number of unofficial strikes which the union leaders could do little to
control, and the general public began to feel irritation with
the unions. A demand grew up for trade union reform—for
example, a ballot of members before a strike, and some urged
that unofficial strikes should be made illegal. Industrial relations remained unsettled, and the trade unions occupied
the limelight, all the more so when in addition there was for
a time communist control of one of the large unions, the
Electrical Trades Union, maintained by fraud in rigging
union elections. The trade union movement, with over ten
million members, stands out as a great power within the
state, almost as a state within the state; their block membership of the Labour Party is five and a half million compared
with only 750,000 individual members. Their power to
force up wages, and so prices, appears a principal producer
of inflation. And both the Labour governments of Harold
Wilson and the Conservative government which followed
have tried to deal with the unions and the problem of strikes.
The Labour policy for the reform of collective bargaining
expressed in its White Paper *In Place of Strife (1969)*, was
withdrawn under union pressure. The Conservatives aimed,
in their Industrial Relations Bill of December 1970, to establish a new legal framework for industrial relations, including
the enforceability of written collective agreements, regula-
tions for registration of trade unions, a National Industrial
Relations Court with power to award compensation against
unions acting illegally, civil proceedings against the leaders
of unofficial strikes, and the reorganisation of the Commission on Industrial Relations (set up by the Labour
Government). These proposals led to a bitter struggle between
Government and the unions.

13. Nationalisation—Socialism Fulfilled?

So it seems that the history of socialism in Britain has
come to an end, that socialism can be regarded as an episode,
an episode finished and complete in itself. This does not
necessarily mean the end of the Labour Party, though even
that has been hinted at—"the kind of slow but sure decline
which—deservedly—affects parties that have ceased to serve
any distinctive political purpose". That was the fate which,
in 1960, Dr Miliband was expecting for a Labour Party
deprived of its socialist policy and faith. At the end of his
Parliamentary Socialism—a clearly written and useful book
though with a strong leftward slant—he was driven to con-
clude that they were faced with the basic question "whether
the Labour Party is to be concerned with attempts at a more
efficient and more humane administration of a capitalist
society; or whether it is to adapt itself to the task of creating
a socialist one". Subsequent events—the elections of 1964
and 1966—have shown that Labour can win victories without socialism, and even its defeat in 1970 left it a powerful
party. As we have seen already, Dr Haseler regarded
Gaitskell's making the Labour Party a non-doctrinaire alternative to Conservatism, that is to say a non-socialist alternative, as the means by which Labour was able to win its
electoral victories under Harold Wilson.

But if socialism has disappeared from Labour Party policy,
if the socialism which once filled a thousand meetings and
a thousand manifestos is heard of no more, what has become of it? What has happened to socialism? Has socialism
been fulfilled? Or has it been betrayed? Was the Labour
Party ever a socialist party? Or has socialism, like so many
social panaceas, proved an illusion?

It might be argued that socialism has been fulfilled. Indeed
in one sense it had been fulfilled—but not as the socialists
had supposed and intended, not by a complete transfer of
private industry to the state. What had happened was that

the historical evolution of society had led to a much greater public control of economic and social life, as Sidney Webb was indicating as early as the *Fabian Essays* of 1889. Attlee and Morrison were, as we have seen, satisfied with the achievements of the Labour Government of 1945. An important programme of nationalisation was carried out, and the welfare state established. Wages rose, there was full employment, there was general prosperity—there was a much higher standard of life, secondary education for all, opportunity open to all. Yet the welfare state was the policy of the Liberal Party as much as that of Labour : Lloyd George had laid the foundations, and Labour policy was based on the famous wartime Beveridge Report, the work of a Liberal. And the affluent society—the modern complement of the welfare state—was as much a characteristic of the period of Conservative government as of the Labour. And behind all this was the work of another Liberal, J. M. Keynes. Born in the year that Karl Marx died, 1883, Keynes was writing in the 1930s to his Fabian friend, Bernard Shaw, about his book *The General Theory of Unemployment, Interest and Money* (1936) which he said would revolutionise economics, as indeed it did. Governments found new techniques—somewhat as Douglas Jay had suggested in 1937—of vastly improving the life of the community *without* any revolutionary taking over of the capitalist system.

Left-wing Labour men incline to the theory of betrayal, betrayal by the leaders. Of the 1945 Labour victory, D. N. Pritt has observed, "If the parliament was largely left-wing, the Government was overwhelmingly right-wing"; he described the new Labour members "who had come with real socialist principles" and said that "the gradual reshaping (called by the Nazis *Gleichshaltung* and by more recent pests brain-washing) to which their leaders subjected them in order to turn them into well-disciplined, anti-Soviet, anti-communist, and non-socialist lobby-fodder, was one of the saddest things I watched in the following four and a half-years". And more recently—as reported from the Labour Party Black-pool conference in October 1970—an appeal for left-wing socialism raised a cheer from the delegates much to the em-barrassment of the leadership.

From the left-wing point of view, nationalisation took place over too narrow a field. It was not the transformation of the whole social system to which socialists had looked for-ward so long; it was not the transfer of power from the old employing class to the working class. Only certain industries —and on the whole industries which were not very profitable —were nationalised, and what have been termed "the com-manding heights" of private industry, that is the highly profitable sections, were left in private hands. Then, instead of socialist control by the workers themselves, the newly-nationalised industries were staffed by very much the same kind of people as before, by people of business experience and managing ability. There was, too, the problem of the compensation to be paid to the previous owners—the share-holders—and this problem was solved to the satisfaction of the owners; at least there was no serious opposition by the Conservatives to the nationalisation measures. The old type of socialist maintained that the compensation was too gener-ous—confiscation might have been preferred—and that it placed too heavy a burden of debt on the industries con-cerned, which could lead to an accusation that the national-ised industry was running at a loss. To most of these Left-wing criticisms there were, of course, answers—the industries nationalised were old and important industries which were in need of reorganisation, among the workers there were few (as Sir Stafford Cripps pointed out) who were capable of taking over the management of large industries, and a peace-ful taking over of industry was only possible on the basis of proper compensation.

Was the Labour Party ever a genuinely socialist party? Might one even suggest that socialism was something in-vented by the *Daily Mail* and fathered on the Labour Party to frighten the electorate? Mr Alan Beattie of the London School of Economics pointed out that accounts of the Labour Party have been much influenced by the personal involvement of convinced socialists, as in the case of G. D. H. Cole, that more recent research (e.g. of Bealey, Pelling, Poirier) has "revealed a party less coherent, less certain of its future and less explicable in terms of socialist ideology than the later accounts of its own members would suggest". With regard to the socialist principles of 1918—Clause IV of the Constitution (committing the Party to public ownership) and *Labour and the New Social Order*—he says "Whether the socialist principles in these documents were more than a rhetorical declaration of party independence is doubtful; the action of the Labour politicians and the trade unionists in the 1920s, with some exceptions, do not appear to represent socialism as anything more than a vague long-term aim of little relevance to immediate circumstances". Such argument though plausible and interesting, can easily be carried too far. Common ownership in place of private capitalism was steadily pressed for many years. To argue the contrary would be like maintaining that, because faith has today declined, and because members of the Christian church have not always lived up to their high standards, the Christian church never believed in Christianity. It is clear, both from the attitudes of the Labour Party and from the experience of living through the years since 1945, that the policy of socialism in itself produced no spectacular success. Improvements there had been in the standard of life and in the social services— great improvements—but these might well have come with or without the socialist policy. After the first two or three hectic and difficult years after the war, improvement was general, over the world and not only in Britain with her limited number of nationalised industries. And so if the socialism envisaged by the enthusiasts of the Labour Party had not been achieved, and if the socialists had not been betrayed by their leaders, one comes to the possibility that socialism had been an illusion. This is the most plausible explanation : socialism—an illusion. It had been a dream, a dream without reality. Socialism might indeed, at any point in history, have brought about an improvement in the human condition, if men were entirely reasonable, entirely well-meaning, entirely unselfish and co-operative—but men are not like that. Socialists had allowed their humanity to run away with them. There was truth in the saying : "He who is not a socialist before he is thirty has no heart; he who is a socialist after he is thirty has no head." That is why the leaders had appeared to enthusiasts and doctrinaires as traitors. The leaders had not intentionally betrayed their principles. At worst they had permitted their good intentions and their enthusiasm to dull their critical faculties and their better judgement. Then, when they found themselves in power, they were obliged somewhat to draw back : they found that earlier optimistic proposals and promises were not practicable; they were obliged to carry through measures which were practicable, and hence of necessity disappointing to those who aimed at all or nothing.

This does not mean, however, that one can say that nationalisation does not work. What one can say, in the light of experience, is that it has not produced the kind of results that socialists envisaged. It does work—it does not result in the breakdown or ruin of the industry concerned; it is clear that mines or railways, for example, can be run by private industry or by the state. Whether the state runs them better or worse than private industry is another, and very difficult, question. Perhaps it makes little difference. When pressed in the 1920s by students, some of whom believed passionately in socialism and others equally strongly in private enterprise, for an opinion on what difference the nationalisation of the railways would make, J. M. Keynes replied that it would not make 2½d difference! The socialist movement could be compared with the free trade movement. Free traders believed in free trade as passionately as socialists believed in socialism.

Free trade, it was maintained, led to national wealth and would bring international peace; protection would lead to disaster. Then in 1932, after crisis national and international, the government introduced a general tariff—and economic conditions returned to something more normal. Free trade or tariffs—what difference did it make? It has been said that a famous American economist spent a large part of his life studying the free trade protection question, and at the end decided that the importance of the question had been somewhat exaggerated!

A quarter of a century has now elapsed since the Labour Government of 1945 commenced its work of nationalisation. There has been ample time for observation of its working and its results, and a number of expert studies have been made. Mr R. Kelf-Cohen, a former civil servant with much experience of the nationalised industries, wrote his *Nationalisation in Britain*—with the sub-title "The End of a Dogma" —in 1958, and a second edition was called for in 1961. In 1960 Professor W. A. Robson produced his massive and authoritative volume, *Nationalised Industry and Public Ownership*, and within a few months of its publication a second edition was needed. The interest in and importance of the subject was apparent.

Professor Robson writes in the careful and guarded language of the academic, yet the lesson is clear. At best the results of nationalisation have been mixed (like, indeed, those of private enterprise)—"The reader will not find," Professor Robson says of his book, " a picture in black and white, a simple story of success or failure. He will find statements and conclusions about some things which are favourable and about others which are unfavourable. I have never wavered in my belief that nationalisation will not by itself bring about drastic changes in the operation of old established industries, although it may enable improvements to be subsequently made." When he comes to assess the actual performance of the nationalised industries, his conclusions are mixed—good and bad. Nationalisation, he maintains, has made larger amounts of capital available and at lower rates of interest than would otherwise have been the case. "It cannot be said, however, that the best possible service at the least real cost to the community is being provided by the coal industry or the railways, partly because the process of modernisation and re-equipment is not sufficiently advanced, and partly because of the attitudes of the workpeople." Wages and conditions of employment, though not uniformly satisfactory, are better, though "the attitudes of the workpeople have not, I believe, been changed in any fundamental sense by nationalisation. Industrial democracy has been fostered in many ways; but there are no clear signs of the growth of a spirit of public service among the rank and file of the employees in any one of the nationalised industries." Professor Robson saw a general advantage in "the existence of a substantial public sector covering the basic industries providing fuel, power and transport" in that this ensured a higher degree of public control over the whole economy, notably to counteract inflation and to maintain full employment. But it is only fair to note that, since he wrote, inflation has continued apace and also that there is unemployment again.

Of the disappearance of socialism as Labour Party policy, Professor Robson wrote : "A highly important factor which has influenced the Labour Party's change of outlook is a feeling of disillusion with the results of nationalisation. The disillusion is partly due to the fact that socialists expected too much from the mere fact of nationalisation and showed insufficient understanding of the problems concerning development, organisation, management, technology, and labour in the industries taken over." He writes sadly of this, and blames the disillusion on "the persistent denigration of the nationalised industries" by the press, by Conservatives, and by business men. Yet he finds it hard to avoid the conclusion that "it is difficult to believe that there is any inherent virtue today in a policy of further nationalisation as an end in itself, regardless of the industries concerned or the ends in view. It is still more difficult to believe that there would be any large amount of electoral support for such a policy."

Mr Kelf-Cohen, after over half a century of interest in nationalisation, is even more outspoken, in his criticism and disillusion. At Manchester Grammar School in 1911 he proposed in the debating society the motion that "This House approves the Nationalisation of the Railways". At the end of his book he concludes : "Of one thing we can be certain. The enthusiasm and determination which launched the series of massive nationalisation projects between 1945 and 1949 can never be recaptured. We have learnt too much since then. That is why the dogma of extensive public ownership has spent its force and run its course."

He provides, too, some pertinent comments on how this change of attitude has come about and on how it has affected the position of the Labour Party. He points to the rather flimsy optimism of socialists in his young days—"We were content to prove that everything was wrong with the existing set-up. Faults were many and easy to find. But when we turned to alternatives, we talked airily of compensating existing shareholders and setting up a Public Board to run the industry." And how easily the critical sense was lulled to sleep by the idea of public as against private : "There was magic in the words 'Public Board' or 'Public Corporation'. They were to be staffed by selfless men of outstanding ability, devoted to the national interest. We assumed that such men were to be found in large numbers; naturally they had no chance to come forward in the degenerate Capitalist era in which we were living. We also assumed that the workers in the industries would be transformed by the Act of Nationalisation and devote themselves to the national interest. Thus the combination of selfless management and selfless workers would bring about the brave new world of Socialism—so utterly different from Capitalism." A lifetime's experience taught him otherwise. He saw Gaitskell as right in his attack

on the socialist dogma of Clause IV, and his nominal defeat
on this issue was due to the strength of the socialist tradition
—"For the zealots of the Party, Socialism must mean public
ownership on a massive scale; weaken the dogma by turning
it into a nicely calculated more or less, and the whole of their
creed is destroyed". Turning the dogma into a nicely calculated more or less was just what Professor Robson did, and
he recognised that one could not any longer expect for
nationalisation "any large amount of electoral support". Mr
Kelf-Cohen came also to this conclusion. He recognised, as
early as 1961, that though the Labour Party was still "mouth-
ing catch phrases and shibboleths" the dogma was at an end.
"Each year that passes," he wrote, "makes it more certain
this country will not tolerate more nationalisation. Any Party
which refuses to recognise this fact counts itself out."

The intellectuals in the Labour Party had, long before
this, realised the profound difficulties in regard to socialist
policy. Their anxiety appeared with the publication in 1952
of *New Fabian Essays* which, with a typically British love of
compromise and sense of continuity, looked back to the
original *Fabian Essays* of 1889 and at the same time virtually
commemorated the end of the old Fabian policy of socialism.
The book had its preface by Attlee, but it was edited by Mr
R. H. S. Crossman (a future Labour minister) and the contributors were mainly of the younger generation of Labour
MPs who had, as Attlee put it, to answer the question
"Where do we go from here?"

Mr Crossman, in the opening essay, frankly admitted the
malaise. "Even before the 1950 election, the impetus which
brought the Labour Government to power began to fail. That
impetus, despite a sharp setback in 1931, had mounted
steadily during fifty years of opposition—years spent in a
sustained campaign against the capitalist order. Yet, after
scarcely four years in office, the Government had fulfilled its
historic mission." And he continued, "Even if the Labour
Government in 1950 had won a large parliamentary major-

ity, the advance to socialism would have been halted". There were, he maintained "symptoms of a much more serious ailment, a failure of the sense of direction. . . . The Labour Party was unsure where it was going. The familiar landmarks on the road to socialism had been left behind." There was, he thought, a real danger : "We have seen, in Australia and New Zealand, what happens to labour parties which dispense with socialism. Now we ourselves are faced with a similar danger—that our socialism may degenerate into labourism." Something new was needed, or at least some revision of the old socialism.

One of the best exponents of revisionism was the young Labour MP, C. A. R. Crosland. His changed attitude to the old socialist policy of nationalisation appears in "The Transition from Capitalism", his contribution to *New Fabian Essays*, and in his *Future of Socialism* (1956) and *The Conservate Enemy* (1962), which put forward a suggested programme of radical reform for the 1960s.

Mr Crosland showed that capitalism, far from collapsing as Marxists had expected, had continued to expand, but that it had itself changed, under pressure from the Left and by reason of technical and administrative change, fuller appreciation of the economic situation, and the effect of two world wars. Very important was the understanding of the Keynes techniques for bringing about full employment—for capitalists, as well as workers, suffer from economic depression and it is to their interest to use the new methods to avoid slumps. The rise of the middle class has upset the old Marxist concept of the class-war, and a middle class way of life has spread far outside that class. In other words, there is now in Britain (as in Scandinavia after years of Labour Government) a new kind of society, a mixed society, not wholly capitalist and not wholly socialist. What has happened is not, as socialists used to think, that capitalism collapsed and was inevitably replaced by socialism, but that capitalism has been transformed into something else, much more reasonable and generally acceptable. What, then, does Labour do now? Mr Crosland thinks that there is still a socialism to be worked for, different from the present mixed system. He ruled out the traditional "nationalisation of the means of production, distribution and exchange" and also the early Fabian collectivism, and put his emphasis on an approximate social and economic equality—the classless society. In spite of all the improvements of the mixed economy, he thinks that Britain is still a class society, and for him "the purpose of socialism is quite simply to eradicate this sense of class, and to create in its place a sense of common interest and equal status." Yet how is this to be achieved? There are great obstacles in the way—gross inequality in the ownership of property, the educational system, and the organisation of industry where "sole rights still belong to the functionless shareholder, and this knowledge still breeds frustration and annoyance among the workers". Mr Crosland is vague about the measures to be taken. He mentions very radical measures, including even the possibility of "a large-scale extension of nationalisation". But this is where we came in—we started with the disillusion over nationalisation, and surely nationalisation is not to be advocated all over again. The doubts and the vagueness about the very fundamentals of socialist policy are indicative of the profound difficulty involved. Disunity and uncertainty are characteristic of the present position. As Mr Crosland put it, in *The Future of Socialism*, "For the first time for a century there is equivocation on the Left about the future of nationalisation".

So much then for nationalisation. There had been a reorganisation of the capitalist system, a partial shift from private capitalism to state capitalism. But socialism had not been fulfilled, not at least fulfilled in the way the socialists had hoped and expected. Yet the idea has lingered on like a pale ghost of its former self. An organisation known as the Socialist Party of Great Britain advertises its aim of "building a world community . . . based on common ownership—with production solely for use—not profit". However, the question arises whether it is right to equate socialism too exclusively with common ownership or nationalisation. There is a sense in which socialism has been thrust, and is still being thrust, on us by forces beyond our control, by the historical development of industrial society which has been going on ever since the Industrial Revolution. The mixed economy of today— or the capitalism of today, if we call it that—is very different from the capitalism of the early nineteenth century, the period of individualism and *laissez faire*. The state has come to take an ever larger part in the control of men's lives. Just as conditions in the early industrial slums—with the danger of cholera and typhoid to rich as well as poor—forced *laissez faire* governments to act despite their own principles and introduce legislation to deal with sanitation and public health, just as the growth of population and industry's need for workers with at least elementary education forced governments to make a public provision of schools, so in time the state has come to exercise a greater control in every sphere. The influence of Keynes helped powerfully to transform the official attitude to economic problems, the government in the White Paper of 1944 accepted responsibility for maintaining a high level of employment, and with the growth of public services and the post-war nationalisation of important industries the actual involvement of the state in the economy became very great. The management of the economy came to be thought of as the proper task of government—though, in spite of Keynes, as events have shown, a task of great difficulty. As the *Observer* pointed out, in a leading article dealing with the budget of 1971, "looming and lowering over everything else, is the unsolved problem of the management of the economy; unless it is solved it will wreck this Government as it wrecked its predecessor".

Thus the state has come to occupy a position in our lives which would have been unthinkable in the early days of individualism. The functions of the state have grown in all directions, there has been a great expansion of bureaucracy, and a great and ever-increasing state expenditure, both central and local. Some people feel that this is leading to men being less ready to stand on their own feet, and expecting the state to do everything for them. Yet life today is so complicated, the pressure of numbers so great, and the size of our problems so vast that control and planning by central organisations is inescapable. In this sense socialism is, today, ever with us—but it is not the socialism of one party with a distinctive socialist policy, but a policy of control and management which every party has necessarily to use. The most serious economic problem of the present is inflation. And it is not inconceivable that the state will find it necessary to curb the freedom of trade unions and employers to make their own wage agreements—this again would be state control, but not the kind of socialism envisaged by socialists.

PART V

RE-APPRAISAL OF SOCIALISM

14. Socialism in Britain and the World

WITH SOCIAL AND economic circumstances radically changed, re-appraisal of socialist theory became necessary, and indeed an agonising re-appraisal has been taking place ever since the end of the government brought into power by the great Labour victory of 1945. Right across the board socialist theory had run up against hard facts : the revolution which so many had expected never came; when a revolution did occur it occurred in the wrong place—in backward, peasant Russia instead of in an industrialised country such as Britain, Germany, or America; when a socialist party at length achieved power by parliamentary means in Britain, the new Keynesian economics was making it possible for capitalism itself to achieve many of the things for which socialists had worked; and, perhaps, worst of all, the two great socialist countries in the world, Russia and China, had shown themselves no better—many would say much worse— in their behaviour and international relations than the worst of the old imperialist powers. Socialism proved to be no royal road to the new millennium.

Things had, in fact, turned out very differently from what the socialists expected. Just as the Victorian who accepted the capitalist order looked for a steady and automatic progress towards a better world, under the influence of increasing wealth, material prosperity, free trade, and world peace, so the socialist came to expect the automatic achievement of socialism through the decay of capitalism, through exploitation and poverty, the formation of a working class movement, and the transformation by the government of the capitalist system into a new socialist society. Neither expectation was fulfilled. Victorian complacency was shaken by the Boer War, and received a final blow in 1914. Socialist assurance suffered blow after blow, and came up against what seemed an insurmountable obstacle when it faced, by the 1950s, the affluent society. Capitalism had compromised, capitalism had reformed itself and produced a way of life tolerable, indeed acceptable and welcome, to the working classes, by removing the conditions—unemployment and poverty—on which socialism had thrived. Still more, the affluent society had destroyed—or gravely weakened—the socialist psychology by depriving the old terms—worker, working class, Labour, even socialism itself—of the old meaning. Much of their emotive force was gone, their emotional power and religious appeal, and they began to fade into the limbo of forgotten things. It was difficult to know any more what the working class was when the workers ran their own cars and went for their holidays by air to the Costa Brava. Mr Jay suggested that the name Labour Party might no longer have reality. And the travel agency, The Workers Travel Association, had for commercial reasons to change its name to World Travel Association—the workers were repelled rather than attracted by the old title. The Labour Government of 1945, then, in spite of its measures of nationalisation, marked not the beginning of a new era of socialist realisation but the end of the period of socialist hope and expectation.

How different the post-war world has proved from the world of the 1920s and 1930s only those who have lived through the whole period can fully appreciate. And those who have lived through it will also know how little they could foresee, in the 1930s, the changes which were to come. The vast increase in population—some eighty million in the

USA and some ten million in Great Britain—was hardly expected; there was, before the war, talk of the danger of under-population due to falling birth rate. High wages, full employment, the spread of education, the great increase in the number of students and of new universities, the welfare state, in spite of all, new problems of juvenile delinquency, crime, and violence, the immense development of air and motor travel and the decline of the railways—all these things came on us, more or less, by surprise. The affluent society itself was a surprise. Accustomed to the enduring economic depression of the 1930s men could hardly but expect that the end of the war—as had indeed happened with earlier wars, the First World War and the Napoleonic Wars—would be followed by renewed depression. There was towards the end of the war—when everyone was fully employed—a half-humorous, half-serious reference to the danger of "peace breaking out". Even Keynes, it is said, half expected a depression in America which would have its dangerous repercussions on this country.

But in the years which followed the war the affluent society became a fact. Socialists themselves—or certainly many socialists, and for the most part the leaders—accepted it. These attempted to bring about revision in socialist theory, and to seek new objectives, or objectives expressed in a different way, and, if they used the term socialism at all, to give it a new appeal. Others would try to see the affluent society as a myth, to seek out and publicise the corners where poverty and hardship still lingered; or they might regard the affluent society as a short-term phenomenon which would bring its own crisis to which a socialist reorganisation of society would prove a solution. For the time being, however, facts spoke for themselves: full employment, high wages, material conditions and a standard of life which had never before been known in this country.

Socialists had thought that there were inherent contradictions in capitalism. They had supposed that capitalist production led inevitably to over-production, that the capitalists produced more goods than the workers with their low wages could buy, and hence there were gluts, unemployment, stagnation, and the attempt to dispose of surplus production abroad which gave rise to imperialism and to war. Slump followed boom in an inevitable trade cycle. Mr John Strachey had held such views, as he says in a most interesting contribution to *New Fabian Essays*, but began to change them about 1938 under the influence of Keynes and Douglas Jay's *The Socialist Case*. And later he came to the conclusion that the Labour Government of 1945 had, in fact, so modified capitalism as to make it workable—the mass unemployment, "the most painful of our social problems before the war", had disappeared. The British economy was no longer stagnant; a great increase in annual production had taken place since the 1930s. But other capitalist nations, notably the USA had also experienced a great economic recovery— and, therefore, one cannot attribute recovery, since America was not socialist, to Britain's particular socialist measures. What happened, it seems, in both cases—in Britain and America—was a redistribution of the national income in one way or another, by higher wages and welfare state social services, by the New Deal and a more progressive system of taxation in America, by guaranteed prices to farmers. Capitalism, that is to say, was able to reform itself, the contradictions were overcome, the balance was redressed between the poorer and richer sections of the community. This new economy of reformed capitalism appeared to Mr Strachey to be the right, the only, course for Britain. In other words, as he put it, "disaster for Britain must result from attempts either to go back to unreformed capitalism or to plunge into full socialism by Leninist methods".

Mr Crossman took a rather different view in a Fabian lecture, published in 1960. He accepted the affluent society, but argued that it could not last. Speaking of the Conservative victories since 1951 he agreed that "there is one thing on which all observers agree. The Government won because a great majority of the voters (including many who voted Labour) accepted Mr Macmillan's contention that they had never had it so good." He recognised that some Labour Party economists were adopting a revisionist position—"Mr Roy Jenkins, Mr Douglas Jay, and Mr C. A. R. Crosland predict that Labour will decline into a minority party, representing an ever shrinking working class, unless it scraps its old-fashioned *critique* of capitalism and modernises its policies". And he cited Mr Jenkins as regarding in particular, among obstacles to Labour recovery, the widespread feeling that Labour was a narrow, class party, and with it the unpopularity of nationalisation. If he were as confident as Mr Crosland in the new, managed capitalism, Mr Crossman went on to say, "I should decide that the Labour Party as such had no further role to play and the time had come to reconstruct the Liberal Party as the main alternative to Conservatism". But Mr Crossman was not as confident as Mr Crosland; instead he saw the communist countries with their planned economies beginning to overtake the wealthy, and too comfortable countries of the West, and he saw the possibility of their demonstrating the victory of nationalisation over free enterprise "before the 1960s are out". He pointed to the danger of Africa, Asia, the Middle East, and South America passing into the communist bloc, and the North Atlantic area becoming a backwater. In place of the old contradictions in the new capitalism—"the price which the modern managed capitalism pays for avoiding the old-fashioned crisis of mass unemployment is the continuous sacrifice of public services, community welfare and national security to private profit". He maintained that the dynamo keeping the affluent society going was the car industry, and referred with approval to the ironical observation that the security of the whole Western world "depends on whether the American people can be persuaded each year to consume six million new cars. If, in any year, that figure falls to four

7—SIB *

million, there is a sharp recession; if to two million, a (non-Communist) world slump." In other words, in the capitalist countries today we spend too much, and invest too little. (Whereas, one might say, during the 1930s' depression we saved too much and did not spend enough. The secret—which no government has found—is to find the proper middle course between the two.) The Labour Party, he argues, must make a socialist challenge to the affluent society, must make the public sector dominant over the private.

Mr Crossman argued plausibly enough. But writing in 1960 he declared: "In my view the kind of Labour Party which they [Messrs Crosland, Jenkins, and Jay] would like to see would fail even in its narrow object of winning the next election. But, much more important, it would be incapable of fulfilling its role as the saviour of our democratic freedoms which may be forced upon it by history before the 1960s are out." A cataclysmic touch here, and again that phrase "before the 1960s are out"! Since he wrote, the Labour Party without—or with precious little—socialism, has won two elections. The 1960s are out, the Labour Party has lost the election of 1970, and in the affluent society the fundamental uncertainties as to Labour policy remain.

In the wider sphere of world affairs the development of Soviet Russia proved both an example and a warning to British socialists. Though Russia, with her socialist economy, has made great economic and technical progress since the 1930s, what happened under the tyranny of Stalin was the very opposite of what British socialists would have hoped and expected from socialism. It is clear that Mr Crossman, torn between his respect for state control and planning and his belief in freedom and democracy, feared in the economic success of the communist bloc a threat to the democratic west. And because Russia and China have proved to be totalitarian states in subjecting their subjects to all-embracing state control through their communist parties, Britain found herself, even under a Labour Government, and despite protests from the left, on the side, not of the Russians and Chinese with their socialist systems but, of the USA and the other countries of NATO.

The experience and misgivings of Citrine about Russia, in the 30s, have been repeated a thousandfold since then. What happened, as exemplified in the lives of individuals, has been told through the experience of six communists or communist sympathisers in *The God that Failed*. What all six of the contributors had in common was that they had all felt the pull of the Communist Party and all suffered a shattering disillusion. "I kept hearing and reading about Soviet Russia," wrote the young Louis Fischer, an American journalist and later a famous writer on Russian affairs. "The Bolsheviks glorified the common man and offered him land, bread, peace, a job, a house, security, education, health, art and happiness. They championed the international brotherhood of the toiling man. They would abolish racial discrimination, exploitation, inequality, the power of wealth, the rights of kings, the lust for territory. . . . The oppressed of the world and the friends of the oppressed saw the Soviets as heralds of a new historic era." Then, as a journalist working in Russia, "the construction of huge factories, hydro-electric power stations, and towns enthused me the more since I looked at it through the magnifying glass of hope. This was but the initial instalment of a grandiose programme which would change the face and raise the living standards of an unfortunate country. . . . Statistics of industrial growth now commenced to fill the Soviet press. They were the music of Socialism, the overture to the new society . . . the mammoth tractor factory in Kharkov . . . the Dnieprostroi dam . . . the collectivisation of agriculture."

Then came second thoughts. The peasants were driven by force into the collectives; they resisted, and livestock and crops suffered; "in the Ukraine these circumstances produced the famine of 1931-2 which killed several million people. Whole villages died. The price of Bolshevik haste and dogmatism was enormous." Stalin established a powerful personal dictatorship, reducing the Communist Party to an obedient rubber stamp—anybody who was suspected of unorthodoxy "received a 2 am visit from the secret police and soon joined the involuntary 'builders of Socialism' in Siberia and the Arctic wastes". Then came the Moscow trials of 1936, 1937 and 1938 : "In their course, the public would be shown only a very tiny fraction of those many thousands whose death, without trial, from a shot in the back of the neck in GPU cellars, beat a shrill discord to the official hosannahs for the new 'Stalin Constitution' "—the constitution, incidentally, so much admired by the Webbs. Later, during the Civil War in Spain, where he was the first American to join the International Brigade, Fischer discovered that the Russians who fought in Spain were executed or disappeared when they returned home—Stalin could tolerate nobody whose communism was not entirely subordinate to him. For Fischer, the breaking point with communism came when Stalin made his pact with Hitler in 1939, precipitating the war. For others the final breaking point came, as he says, when Russia attacked Finland at the end of the same year.

The purges and spectacular public trials under Stalin did indeed astonish the world. The casualty lists of those disposed of by Stalin contained names widely known. There were the names of those who made the revolution in 1917— famous names in Russia, Zinoviev. Kamenev, Bukharin, Marshal Tukhachevsky. Trotsky's name was not there, for he had been exiled in 1929, and was assassinated in Mexico in 1940. These Russian leaders were hysterically accused of every sort of political crime—treachery, fascism, counter-revolution, espionage, sabotage. If they were guilty what a country was Russia in which such men had for years held high positions; if they were innocent, how monstrous indeed was the dictatorship of Stalin. In either case, the light thrown on the world's first socialist state discovered a situation fraught with warning for the rest of the world not least for socialists themselves.

The situation would have been bad enough if the rest of the world had been calm and safe. Yet this was the very time when Nazi Germany was re-arming itself for the domination of the world. There should have been a collective effort to resist Nazi aggression by Britain, France, and Russia. It is true that Britain and France were inclined to appeasement, but one reason—or at least excuse—for this policy was that no reliance could be put on a government like that of Soviet Russia. Indeed, to quote Fischer again, "A democratic Russia would have helped anti-appeasement forces in England and France unseat their Neville Chamberlains and Daladiers. . . . A democratic Russia, in other words, might have prevented the war which the totalitarian Soviets helped to precipitate."

If Russia precipitated the war, by an extraordinary irony she also won it. Without the mighty effort of the Red Army, Britain and America could not have conquered Hitler. Yet in spite of the official friendly relations of the war-time alliance, as soon as the war was over Russia followed her own way in isolation. Labour Governments found it no easier to work with Russia than did Conservative ones. Russia was unwilling to co-operate in the control of occupied Germany, and subjected Poland and the whole of south-eastern Europe to communist domination. The Cold War developed. It looked as though Russia might overrun Western Europe, until the Western powers first adopted the Marshall Plan for economic reconstruction and then formed NATO in self defence. In the Far East the challenge of communism came to open war with the attack made by communist North Korea on South Korea, resulting in a three years war. Only the death of Stalin in 1953 brought relief, and the easing of the situation in Russia—Russia's new ruler, Khrushchev, denounced the Stalinist tyranny, and Stalin's embalmed body was removed from its place of honour alongside that of

Lenin in Red Square. But there were new crises to come : the Russians suppressed by force an attempt by Hungary to break loose from their control, there was an acute danger when Russia prepared to set up a missile base in communist Cuba, and in 1968 a Russian invasion destroyed the effort to create a liberal regime in Czechoslovakia. To many people all over the world—many of them socialists—communist Russia appeared almost as great a threat as totalitarian Germany had ever been. Meanwhile a communist regime had been established in China also—with violence, bloodshed, and executions inside, and an attitude of hatred and isolation towards the outside world.

Wrangles—and the danger of war—now arose between the two great socialist countries of the world, Russia and China. To China, Russia appeared to be revisionist, and was accused of betraying the revolution.

Communists and socialists have always been known for their failure to agree. Bernstein, who modified the doctrines of Marx, was the first revisionist, and the revisions have gone on ever since. As we have seen there are fundamental disagreements in the British Labour Party on their socialist policy. Disagreements abroad have been fiercer and more numerous—ex-communists disagree bitterly with communists. It has been said, indeed, that the final battle will be between communists and ex-communists. In Britain, perhaps, we may expect the final battle to be between the socialists and ex-socialists.

Bibliography

BIBLIOGRAPHY

General

For source material see G. D. H. Cole and A. W. Filson: *British Working Class Movements—Select Documents 1789-1875* (Macmillan 1951). Another collection—from a Marxist point of view—is *History in the Making* (Lawrence and Wishart, 1948), vol. 1 Max Morris (ed): *From Cobbett to the Chartists 1815-1848*, vol. 2 J. B. Jefferys (ed): *Labour's Formative Years 1849-1879*, vol. 3 E. J. Hobsbawm (ed): *Labour's Turning Point 1880-1900*.

The amount of writing on socialism and allied subjects is immense, and this bibliography can only offer a selection. Max Beer: *History of British Socialism* (2 vols., Bell 1919, '20) is an established classic. Some of the older histories, by Thomas Kirkup and Dr Shadwell, have their own character and value. Useful modern works are A. Gray: *The Socialist Tradition—Moses to Lenin* (Longmans 1946), G. Lichtheim: *Origins of Socialism* (Weidenfeld & Nicolson 1969), the encyclopaedic H. W. Laidler: *History of Socialism* (Routledge 1968), an excellent short survey, N. Mackenzie: *Socialism* (Hutchinson 1966), and E. P. Thompson: *The Making of the English Working Class* (Gollancz 1965). The many works of G. D. Cole include a comprehensive *History of Socialist Thought* (5 vols., Macmillan (1953-60), vol. 1 *The Forerunners 1789-1850*, vol. 2 *Marxism ad Anarchism 1850-1890*, vol. 3 (in 2 parts) *The Second International 1889-1914*, vol. 4 (in 2 parts) *Communism and Social Democracy 1914-1931*, vol. 5 *Socialism and Fascism 1931-1939*, His *Short History of the British Working-Class*

Movement 1789-1947 (Allen and Unwin, new edition 1947) is also useful.

Three brief and compact accounts are H. Pelling: *A Short History of the Labour Party* (Macmillan 1961), *A History of British Trade Unionism* (Macmillan 1963), and *The British Communist Party* (Black 1958). See also C. F. Brand: *The British Labour Party* (Stanford University Press 1965).

1. The Industrial Revolution

Especially useful are T. S. Ashton: *The Industrial Revolution* (OUP 1948), and an introductory essay, H. L. Beales: *The Industrial Revolution 1750-1850* (Cass 1958). In the background are the standard works of Mantoux, Clapham, Arnold Toynbee, Lilian Knowles, C. R. Fay, and J. L. and B. Hammond. Recent books are Phyllis Deane: *The First Industrial Revolution* (CUP 1965); R. M. Hartwell (ed): *Causes of the Industrial Revolution in England* (Methuen 1967) and R. M. Hartwell (ed.): *The Industrial Revolution* (Blackwell 1970). A general, vivid account of the period is E. J. Hobsbawm: *The Age of Revolution 1789-1848* (Weidenfeld and Nicolson 1962).

For the working class movements of the time a most useful guide is J. T. Ward (ed): *Popular Movements* c. *1830-1850* (Macmillan 1970), a series of essays, covering recent research and with invaluable bibliographies, on parliamentary reform, the factory reform movement, the anti-Poor Law agitation, trade unionism, Chartism, and the agitation against the Corn Laws. Books calling for special mention are Asa Briggs (ed): *Chartist Studies* (Macmillan 1959), G. D. H. Cole: *Chartist Portraits* (Macmillan 1965), and *Attempts at General Union* (Macmillan 1953); also, for the Chartist left wing, A. R. Schoyen: *The Chartist Challenge* (Heinemann 1958)—a life of George Julian Harney, and J. Saville: *Ernest Jones* (Lawrence and Wishart

1956). Engels' *Condition of the Working Class in England in 1844,* has been edited by W. O. Henderson and W. H. Chaloner (Blackwell 1958), and Harney's Chartist journal, *Red Republican* (1850-51) has been republished with an introduction by John Saville (Merlin Press 1966). *An Anthology of Chartist Literature* (Central Books) is a collection, published in Moscow 1956, of extracts from journals and tracts, *The Northern Star, The Chartist Circular, The Labourer, The Red Republican, The Friend of the People,* and others.

2. Robert Owen

The Life of Robert Owen (Wilson 1857)—written by himself, but takes his life only to 1822. *A New View of Society* (1813-14) is printed in an appendix. Vol. 1A of the *Life* (1858) includes material Owen selected for the years 1803-20, including his *Report to the committee of the Association for the relief of the manufacturing and labouring poor* (1817) and his *Report to the County of Lanark* (1820) Robert Dale Owen: *Threading My Way* (Trübner & Co. 1874) is an autobiography by Owen's son.

For a list of books, pamphlets, and periodicals, by Owen and the Owenites, see the bibliography published by the National Library of Wales (1925), and the bibliography in J. F. C. Harrison (below).

F. Podmore: *Robert Owen* (Hutchinson 1906) was for long the standard life. G. D. Cole: *Life of Robert Owen* (Macmillan 1930) is a useful biography. An important recent book is J. F. C. Harrison: *Robert Owen and the Owenites in Britain and America* (Routledge 1969). Cole's *Attempts at General Union,* A. E. Bestor: *Backwoods Utopias* (University of Pennsylvania Press 1950), and W. H. G. Armytage: *Heavens Below* (Routledge 1961) also deal with aspects of Owen's work. Bestor's book, sub-titled "the Sectarian and Owenite Phases of Communitarian Socialism in America 1663-1829" contains full bibliographical information. See also J. Butt (ed): *Robert Owen* (David & Charles 1971).

3. Other Socialistic Voices

Lord John Manners: *England's Trust and Other Poems* (Rivington 1841); Samuel Wilberforce: *A Charge delivered to the Clergy* (James Burns 1840); J. S. Mill: *Principles of Political Economy* (Parker 1848, 2nd ed, 1949); *Autobiography* (Longmans 1873). There were various social betterment movements which were not socialist, e.g. The Labourers' Friend Society, which, under royal patronage, arranged the letting of allotments to labourers. See its publications, *Labourers' Friend Magazine* (1834-38) and *The Labourers' Friend* (1835).

Politics for the People Ludlow and Maurice (eds), in 1848; in book form (Parker 1848); *Tracts on Christian Socialism* (Bell 1850); *The Christian Socialist* (1850-52). F. M. Maurice: *The Kingdom of Christ* (Darton & Clark 1837); Charles Kingsley: *Alton Locke*; *Yeast*; *Cheap Clothes and Nasty* (printed with *Alton Locke*); *Sermons on the Cholera* (printed in *Sermons on National Subjects*). See *Collected Works* (Macmillan 1880-82).

Works of John Ruskin, E. T. Cook and A. Wedderburn (eds) (George Allen 1903-12) vol. 18 contains *Unto this Last*, *Munera Pulveris* ("Gifts of the Dust"—a somewhat cryptic title), *Time and Tide*, and other writings on economic subjects. *Fors Clavigera* ("Fortune the Nail-bearer") in vols. 27-29. Vol. 30 is devoted to the Guild of St George.

C. E. Raven: *Christian Socialism 1848-54* (Macmillan 1920. New impression 1968) and T. Christensen: *Origin and History of Christian Socialism 1848-54* (University of Aarhus 1962) deal with the movement, and there are lives of the principal figures—Una Pope-Hennessy: *Canon Charles Kingsley* (Chatto & Windus 1948); C. W. Stubbs:

Charles Kingsley and the Christian Social Movement (Blackie 1899); J. F. Maurice: *Life of Frederick Denison Maurice* (Macmillan 1884); H. G. Wood: *Frederick Denison Maurice* (CUP 1950); N. C. Masterman: *J. M. F. Ludlow* (CUP 1963).

On Ruskin, there is J. A. Hobson: *John Ruskin, Social Reformer* (Nisbet 1898), and lives by Joan Evans (Cape 1954), and R. H. Wilenski (Faber 1933).

An article which dealt with the topic raised at the close of this chapter is B. Harrison and P. Hollis, "Chartism, Liberalism, and the Life of Robert Lowery" in the *English Historical Review*, 82, 1967.

4. Marx and Marxism

Probably the most useful collection of extracts from the writings of Marx, Engels, Lenin, and Stalin is *A Handbook of Marxism* (ed Emile Burns, Gollancz, 1935). Also *Selected Works*, 2 vols. (Lawrence and Wishart). The 1930 English edition of *The Communist Manifesto* (translated Eden and Cedar Paul, Martin Lawrence) contains an introduction and notes by D. Ryazanoff, Director of the Marx-Engels Institute in Moscow.

Capital (published 1930 by Dent in Everyman's Library. Translated by Eden and Cedar Paul from Book I of *Das Kapital*) has a short and helpful introduction by G. D. H. Cole.

In 1968 there was completed a collected, standard edition of the Karl Marx/Friedrich Engels *Werke* in 39 volumes (plus an additional volume) produced by the Institute for Marxism-Leninism in the German Democratic Republic and published by the Dietz Verlag, Berlin. There is also a Russian edition by the Institute of Marxism-Leninism in Moscow.

From the large number of books on Marx and Marxism, the following is a selection: I. Berlin: *Karl Marx* (OUP

1963); F. Mehring: *Karl Marx* (trans. E. Fitzgerald, John Lane 1936); E. H. Carr: *Karl Marx: a Study in Fanaticism* (Dent 1934); H. J. Laski: *Communism* (Thornton 1927); A. D. Lindsay: *Karl Marx's Capital* (Humphrey Milford 1925); B. Russell: *Freedom and Organization 1814-1914* (Allen and Unwin 1934); G. D. H. Cole: *What Marx Really Meant* (Gollancz 1934) and *The Meaning of Marxism* (Gollancz 1948); S. Hook: *Towards the Understanding of Karl Marx* (Gollancz 1933); Emile Burns: *What is Marxism?* (Gollancz 1939. New revised ed, Lawrence and Wishart 1952).

E. V. Böhm-Bawerk: *Karl Marx and the Close of his System* (T. Fisher Unwin 1898); H. W. B. Joseph: *The Labour Theory of Value in Karl Marx* (O.U.P. 1923); R. N. Carew-Hunt: *The Theory and Practice of Communism* (Bles 1950); B. D. Wolfe: *Three who made a Revolution* (Thames and Hudson 1956), *Marxism—one hundred years in the life of a doctrine* (Chapman and Hall 1967).

5. *Revival of Socialism*

H. M. Hyndman: *The Record of an Adventurous Life* (Macmillan 1911); *The Letters of William Morris* P. Henderson (ed) (Longmans 1950)—contains an excellent photograph of the Socialist League, Hammersmith Branch, with William Morris and his daughters Jennie and May; see also *Collected Works* (Longmans 1910-25), with introductions by May Morris, chiefly *News from Nowhere, A Dream of John Ball*, and *Lectures on Socialism*; E. R. Pease: *History of the Fabian Society* (Fifield 1916); Robert Blatchford: *My Eighty Years* (Cassell 1931), *Merrie England* (Clarion 1894), *Britain for the British* (Clarion Press 1902); *The Labour Party Foundation Conference and Annual Conference Reports 1900-1905* (Hammersmith Reprints, Hammersmith Bookshop Ltd 1967); *The Miners Next Step* (R. Davies,

Tonypandy 1912); *Tom Mann's Memoirs* (Labour Publishing Co. 1923).

H. Pelling: *Origins of the Labour Party 1800-1900* (Macmillan 1954) with an extensive bibliography; F. Bealey and H. Pelling: *Labour and Politics 1900-1906* (Macmillan 1958) with a list of unpublished sources; P. P. Poirier: *The Advent of the Labour Party* (Allen and Unwin 1958); R. E. Dowse: *Left in the Centre: the Independent Labour Party 1893-1940* (Longmans 1966); W. Ashworth: *Economic History of England 1870-1939* (Methuen 1960); R. Blake: Disraeli (Eyre and Spottiswoode 1966); S. MacCoby: *English Radicalism 1853-1886* (Allen and Unwin 1938); Mrs Margaret Cole: *Story of Fabian Socialism* (Heinemann 1961); E. P. Thompson: *William Morris, Romantic to Revolutionary* (Lawrence and Wishart 1955); in A. Briggs and J. Saville (ed): *Essays in Labour History* (Macmillan 1969), E. P. Thompson on "Homage to Tim Maguire" for ILP penetration of trade union branches.

On Syndicatism and Guild Socialism, see G. D. H. Cole: *World of Labour* (Bell 1913), and *Short History of the British Working Class Movement*; Dona Torr: *Tom Mann* (Lawrence and Wishart 1936), and *Tom Mann and his Times* vol. 1 (Lawrence and Wishart 1956); G. D. H. Cole: *Guild Socialism Restated* (Parsons 1920).

6. *Ideas of British Socialism*

Fabian Essays in Socialism (G. Bernard Shaw (ed) 1889).

E. R. Pease and Mrs Cole, as for Chapter 5. Beatrice Webb: *My Apprenticeship* (Longmans 1926) and *Our Partnership* (Longmans 1948); H. Pelling, as for Chapter 5. Also A. M. McBriar: *Fabian Socialism and English Politics 1884-1918* (CUP 1932); Mrs Cole (ed): *The Webbs and their Work* (Muller 1949).

7. Lives of the Socialists

William Stewart: *J. Keir Hardie* (Cassell 1921); D. Lowe: *From Pit to Parliament* (Labour Publishing Co. 1923); Emrys Hughes: *Keir Hardie* (Allen and Unwin 1950); Glanmor Williams (ed): *Merthyr Politics: The Making of a Working-Class Tradition* (University of Wales Press 1966).

Lord Elton: *The Life of James Ramsay MacDonald* (Collins 1939) for the period 1866-1919. Also lives by H. H. Tiltman (Jarrolds, not dated), and Mary Agnes Hamilton (Cape 1929).

Alan Bullock: *Life and Times of Ernest Bevin*, vol. 1 (Heinemann 1960).

James Griffiths: *Pages from Memory* (Dent 1969).

See also Philip Snowden: *An Autobiography* (Ivor Nicholson and Watson 1934); J. H. Thomas: *My Story* (Hutchinson 1937); Lord Morrison: *Herbert Morrison* (Odhams 1960); J. R. Clynes: *Memoirs* (Hutchinson 1937); Mary Agnes Hamilton: *Arthur Henderson* (Heinemann 1938).

8. The War and New Opportunity

Labour Party Bibliography (Labour Party 1967) furnishes a list of party publications. Wartime pamphlets, e.g. *The British Labour Movement and the War*, issued in 1915 by the Labour Party and TUC; *Why British Labour supports the War* (undated) by J. A. Seddon, a former Labour MP and president of the TUC, and *The New Charter for the Workers* (1917—reprinted from *The Herald*); *The New Party Constitution* (1918-19). Memoirs and biographies are especially useful. For Ramsay MacDonald, as for Chapter 7. Viscount Snowden (Philip Snowden): *An Autobiography* (Ivor Nicholson & Watson 1937); Hugh Dalton: *Call Back Yesterday: Memoirs 1887-1931* and *The Fateful Years: Memoirs 1931-45* (Muller 1953, 1957); Fenner Brockway: *Socialism over Sixty Years* (Allen & Unwin 1946) being the life of

F. W. Jowett of Bradford; E. Shinwell: *The Labour Story* (Macdonald 1963); Francis Williams: *Fifty Years' March* (Odhams 1949), that is the rise of the Labour Party. *Beatrice Webb's Diaries 1912-24* (Longmans 1952) Margaret Cole (ed), and *Beatrice Webb's Diaries 1924-32* (Longmans 1956).

G. D. H. Cole: *History of the Labour Party from 1914* (Routledge 1948); H. Pelling: *Short History of the Labour Party*; R. Miliband: *Parliamentary Socialism* (Allen & Unwin 1961); S. H. Beer: *Modern British Politics* (Faber 1965); R. K. Middlemas: *The Clydesiders* (Hutchinson 1965).

R. W. Lyman: *First Labour Government 1924* (Chapman & Hall 1957); L. Chester, S. Fay, and H. Young: *The Zinoviev Letter* (Heinemann 1967).

R. Bassett: *1931: Political Crisis* (Macmillan 1958); R. Skidelsky: *Politicians and the Slump* (Macmillan 1967), for the Labour Government of 1929-31. M. G. Rees: *The Great Slump 1929-33* (Weidenfeld & Nicolson 1970); S. Pollard: *The Gold Standard and Employment Policies between the Wars* (Methuen 1970); H. W. Arndt: *Economic Lessons of the 1930s* (RIIA 1944).

9. Theory and Practice

Labour Party policy statements—*Labour and the New Social Order* (1918); *Labour and the Nation* (1928); *For Socialism and Peace* (1934). *Labour Year Book* (1916 and 1919); *Labour and Capital in Parliament* (Labour Research Department 1923). Labour election manifestos are collected in F. W. S. Craig (ed): *British General Election Manifestos 1918-1966* (Political Reference Publications, Chichester 1970). Party pamphlets, e.g. *The Outlook for Labour*, by Arthur Henderson (Labour Party 1918); *The Mines and the Nation* (reprinted from *Daily Herald* 1920); *The Nationalization of the Coal Industry*, by R. H. Tawney (Labour Party 1919?); *The Mines for the Nation*, by T. I. Mardy Jones and

A. J. Cook (Labour Publications Dept. undated); *The Land For the People—Why public ownership is the key to high wages on the farm* (Labour Party undated); *Youth for Socialism!* (Labour Party League of Youth 1934); *Victory for Socialism—speaker's guide* (Labour Party 1935). *Fabian Essays* (editions of 1920 and 1931); J. Ramsay MacDonald: *Socialism: Critical and Constructive* (Cassell 1921); Hugh Dalton: *The Inequalities of Incomes in Modern Communities* (Routledge 1920); R. H. Tawney: *The Acquisitive Society* (Bell 1921) and *Equality* (Allen & Unwin 1931); John Strachey: *Theory and Practice of Socialism* (Gollancz 1936); Douglas Jay: *The Socialist Case* (Faber 1937); E. F. M. Durbin: *The Politics of Democratic Socialism* (Routledge 1940).

S. H. Beer: *Modern British Politics*, as for Chapter 8, and R. T. Mackenzie: *British Political Parties* (Heinemann 1955).

10. The General Strike

Thomas Jones: *Whitehall Diary* vol. 2 1926-30 K. Middlemas (ed) (OUP 1969); *Beatrice Webb's Diaries 1924-32*. For the early 19th Century idea of the general strike see William Benbow: *Grand National Holiday, and Congress of the Productive Classes* (The Author, London 1832).

Julian Symons: *The General Strike* (Cresset 1959); Alan Bullock: *Ernest Bevin*; W. H. Crook: *The General Strike— A Study of Labor's tragic weapon in theory and practice* (University of North Carolina Press 1931), and *Communism and the General Strike* (Shoe String Press, Hamden, Connecticut 1960). For early ideas of a general strike, see Cole: *Attempts at General Union*; A. J. C. Rüter's introduction to a facsimile of Benbow's pamphlet in *International Review for Social History* (Holland 1936); Niles Carpenter, "William Benbow and the Origin of the General Strike", *Quarterly Journal of Economics*, vol. 35 (May 1921); A. Plummer, "The General Strike during One Hundred Years", *Economic Journal*, Supplement, May 1927.

11. The Russian Influence

Walter Citrine (Lord Citrine): *I search for Truth in Russia* (Routledge 1936); *Men and Work* (Hutchinson 1964) and *Two Careers* (Hutchinson 1967) are his two volumes of autobiography; S. and B. Webb: *Soviet Communism, A New Civilisation?* (Longmans 1953)—two substantial volumes, republished later without the question mark; also their *Truth about Soviet Russia* (Longmans 1944); Beatrice Webb: *Diaries 1924-32* (Longmans 1956); John Strachey: *The Coming Struggle for Power* (Gollancz 1932).

Kitty Muggeridge and Ruth Adam: *Beatrice Webb* (Secker and Warburg 1967); Malcolm Muggeridge: *Winter in Moscow* (Eyre and Spottiswoode 1934), and *The Thirties* (Hamish Hamilton 1940); T. L. Jarman: *Through Soviet Russia* (Houghton 1933); Durbin's *Politics of Democratic Socialism* (1940) pointed out the terrible similarities between the regimes in Soviet Russia and Nazi Germany; S. R. Graubard: *British Labour and the Russian Revolution 1917-1924* (Harvard University Press 1956); R. Conquest: *The Great Terror* (Macmillan 1968).

12. Labour Governments of Attlee and Wilson

C. R. Attlee: *As it happened* (Heinemann 1954); *Purpose and Policy* (Hutchinson 1947)—selected speeches of Attlee; *A Prime Minister remembers* (i.e. Attlee) Francis Williams (ed) (Heinemann 1961); Hugh Dalton: *High tide and after: Memoirs 1945-60* (Muller 1962); D. N. Pritt: *The Labour Government 1945-51* (Lawrence & Wishart 1963).

Pelling, Miliband, and Beer as before. R. B. McCallum and A. Readman: *The British General Election of 1945* (OUP 1947); E. Watkins: *The Cautious Revolution* (Secker & Warburg 1951); R. A. Brady: *Crisis in Britain* (CUP 1950); A. A. Rogow: *The Labour Government and British Industry*

1945-1951 (Blackwell 1955); Roy Harrod : *Are these Hardships necessary?* (Hart Davis 1947); Joan Mitchell : *Crisis in Britain 1951* (Secker and Warburg 1963); G. D. N. Worswick and P. H. Ady (ed) : *The British Economy 1945-1950* (OUP 1952); and *The British Economy in the 1950s* (OUP 1962); A. J. Youngson: *The British Economy 1920-1957* (Allen & Unwin 1960); S. Pollard : *Development of the British Economy 1914-1967* (Arnold 1969); J. C. R. Dow: *The Management of the British Economy 1945-60* (CUP 1964); A. A. Shonfield : *British Economic Policy since the War* (Penguin Books 1958), and *Modern Capitalism* (OUP 1965); M. Stewart: *Keynes and After* (Penguin 1967); R. Lekachman : *The Age of Keynes* (Penguin 1967); Lord Franks *"Evolution of 20th Century Capitalism"* in *The Future of Capitalism* (Macmillan N.Y. 1967); M. Kidron : *Western Capitalism since the War* (Weidenfeld & Nicolson 1968); S. Tsuru (ed): *Has Capitalism changed?* (Shoten, Tokyo 1961); Maurice Bruce : *The Coming of the Welfare State* (Batsford 1961); Allan Flanders : *Trade Unions* (Hutchinson 1963).

S. Haseler : *The Gaitskellites* (Macmillan 1969).

13. Nationalisation

See also the books for Chapter 12. Alan Beattie (ed) : *English Party Politics* (Weidenfeld and Nicolson 1970)—extracts from documents with editorial introductions. Vol. 2 contains a useful section on "The Emergence of Labour 1906-32". W. A. Robson : *Nationalized Industry and Public Ownership* (Allen & Unwin 2nd ed. 1962); R. Kelf-Cohen : *Nationalisation in Britain* (Macmillan 1961); E. E. Barry : *Nationalisation in British Politics* (Cape 1965).

R. H. S. Crossman (ed) : *New Fabian Essays* (Turnstile Press 1952); C. A. R. Crosland : *The Future of Socialism* (Cape 1956); and *The Conservative Enemy* (Cape 1962).

A. Cairncross: *The Managed Economy* (Blackwell 1970).

14. Re-appraisal

Fabian Tracts, chiefly R. H. S. Crossman: *Labour in the Affluent Society* (1960), *Socialism and the New Despotism* (1956); Hugh Gaitskell: *Socialism and Nationalisation* (1956); C. A. R. Crosland: *A social democratic Britain* (Jan. 1971). Also Hugh Gaitskell: *Recent Developments in British Socialist Thinking* (Co-operative Union 1956.)

Arthur Koestler and others: *The God that failed* (Hamish Hamilton 1950)—with introduction by R. H. S. Crossman; Bertrand Russell: *Practice and Theory of Bolshevism* (Allen & Unwin 1920)—a book he was able to republish in 1949, virtually without change.

INDEX

INDEX

Acland, 102

Acts of Parliament

Alexander, A. V., 164

Amery, L. S., 147

Anabaptists, 19

Aquinas, St Thomas, 18

Aristotle, 13, 14–16, 18

Ashton, Professor, 26

Ashworth, Professor, 77

Asquith, H. H., 102, 117, 118, 120, 121, 124

Attlee, C. R., 9, 10, 12, 38, 163, 165, 168, 171, 177, 184; leader of Labour Party, 130

Augustine, St, *De Civitate Dei*, 16

Australia, 9

Babeuf, Gracchus, 21, 35, 36

Bacon, Francis, *New Atlantis*, 16

Bakunin, 66, 116

Baldwin, Stanley, 124, 143, 145–6, 147–8

Ball, John, 19

Barnes, George, 119

Bax, Belfort, 75

Beattie, Alan, 179

Beer, Professor Samuel H., 134

Benbow, William, 141

Benedict, St, 17

Bentham, Jeremy, 40, 41, 55

Berlin, Sir Isaiah, 69

Bernstein, 198

Besant, Annie, 94

Bevan, Aneurin, 38, 154